The Project of Autonomy:
Politics and Architecture w

Pier Vittorio Aureli

MW01281755

A copublication of the Buell Center / FORuM Project
and Princeton Architectural Press

This book is copublished by

The Temple Hoyne Buell Center
for the Study of American Architecture
1172 Amsterdam Avenue
Columbia University
New York, New York 10027
and
Princeton Architectural Press
37 East Seventh Street
New York, New York 10003

Visit our website at www.papress.com

ISBN 978-1-61689-100-8

The Library of Congress has catalogued the
hardcover edition as follows:
Aureli, Pier Vittorio.
 The project of autonomy : politics and
architecture within and against capitalism /
Pier Vittorio Aureli.
88 p., [32] p. of plates : ill. (some col.) ; 23 cm.
— (FORuM project)
Includes bibliographical references.
ISBN 978-1-56898-794-1 (hardcover : alk. paper)
1. Architecture, Modern—20th century. 2.
Architecture, Postmodern. I. Temple Hoyne
Buell Center for the Study of American
Architecture. II. Title.
NA680.A93 2008
724'.6—dc22
                              2008005448

The Project of Autonomy: Politics and
Architecture within and against Capitalism
is the fourth volume in a series of books related
to the FORuM Project, dedicated to exploring
the relationship of architectural form to politics
and urban life. FORuM is a program of The
Temple Hoyne Buell Center for the Study of
American Architecture at Columbia University.

Project conceptualization:
Joan Ockman and Pier Vittorio Aureli
Project coordination:
Sara Goldsmith and Diana Martinez

For the Temple Hoyne Buell Center
Series editor: Joan Ockman
Executive editor: Sara Goldsmith
Editorial assistant: Sharif Khalje
Copy editor: Stephanie Salomon
Designer: Dexter Sinister, New York

For Princeton Architectural Press
Production editor: Linda Lee

Special thanks to:
Sara Bader, Nicola Bednarek Brower,
Janet Behning, Fannie Bushin, Megan Carey,
Carina Cha, Andrea Chlad, Russell Fernandez,
Will Foster, Jan Haux, Diane Levinson,
Jennifer Lippert, Jacob Moore, Katharine
Myers, Margaret Rogalski, Elana Schlenker,
Dan Simon, Sara Stemen, Andrew Stepanian,
Paul Wagner, and Joseph Weston
of Princeton Architectural Press
—Kevin C. Lippert, publisher

Contents

Autonomy and History

In 1989 the Greek-French philosopher Cornelius Castoriadis gave a lecture at Boston University with a significant title: "The Retreat from Autonomy." The core of Castoriadis's lecture was a polemical attack on the widely accepted historical periodization modern/postmodern. Castoriadis objected to this periodization because it provoked an impasse within history's necessary movement of ruptures and revolutions. If the idea of modernity existed only as a prolonged state of the present—which contradicted its explicit pretensions to be the tradition of the new—it also announced the antimodern theme *par excellence:* "the end of history." On the other hand, the idea of postmodernity, as the antithesis of modernity, manifested a pathetic inability to express something positive *tout court,* "leading to its self-definition as simply post-something, that is, through a reference to that which was but is not anymore, and to its attempts at self-glorification by means of the bizarre contention that its meaning is no-meaning and its style is no-style."[1]

Moreover, postmodernity not only eliminated the possibility to take an affirmative position but also the teleological basis necessary to sustain it as such, namely the historical evolution of the emancipatory process of human reason. In so doing, postmodernity brought intellectuals to refuse any totalizing vision of history understood as a process of human liberation. This act of refusal Castoriadis did not consider negative in itself, but in the thinking of the postmodernists it served to eliminate the question "Are all historical periods and all social-historical regimes therefore equivalent?"[2] For Castoriadis, the impossibility of rendering any historical judgment on this question, and indeed of any judgment at all, led "to political agnosticism, or to the funny acrobatics performed by the postmodernists or their brethren when they feel obliged to defend freedom, democracy, human rights, and so on."[3]

In the face of this impasse, Castoriadis proposed a different periodization, one openly founded on an explicitly political preconception of history. His periodization began from the assumption that the distinctiveness of Western thinking consisted of the evolution of the social and individual meanings

4

it attributed to the project of autonomy. By project of autonomy Castoriadis meant the establishing of a relationship between individuals and their knowledge different from the one inherited from previous periods. He accordingly defined three historical moments within the project of autonomy, which he identified as beginning at the end of the "true" Middle Ages: first, the reconstruction of Western thinking; second, the critical period, that is, the modern; and third, the retreat into "conformism."

By reconstruction of Western thinking, Castoriadis meant the rediscovery of political autonomy. This took place on both a practical level—think of the rise of autonomous municipalities starting in the fourteenth century—and also a theoretical level—even if Castoriadis did not mention this important reference, think of Machiavelli's interpretation of politics as liberated from all metaphysical representations and analyzed in terms of immanent "criteria of action." This rediscovery of political autonomy occurred in the context of the systematic reevaluation of Roman law and the whole political, philosophical, and cultural legacy of the Greco-Roman world. A perfect fusion of the innovative developments implicit in this rediscovery and reevaluation, on the one hand, and traditional forms of power such as absolute monarchy and the Church, on the other, became possible in the Hobbesian period of "political classicism" that existed during the seventeenth century.

The critical or modern period extended from the Enlightenment (circa 1750) to the sunset of totalitarianisms (1955–60). According to Castoriadis, this period was characterized by the convergence of two beliefs: in the autonomy of the subject, and in the unlimited expansion of the rationality implicit in technological development. The autonomy of the subject was manifested both in the crisis of traditional governmental models, such as monarchy, and their replacement with new ones (for example, during the French Revolution); and in the creation of new forms in the arts and literature, the validity of which arose not only from what they represented but also, and especially, from their formal constitution. The unlimited expansion of rational mastery of technology had a correlate in the study of the natural sciences. But from the beginning, as Theodor W. Adorno and Max Horkheimer also theorized,

5

rationalism was a mentality immediately appropriated and forwarded by the expanding and totalizing reach of capitalism. Indeed, capitalism was not simply a process of accumulation, but a scientific understanding of capitalism's continuous innovation, its incessant revolution of production, consumption, and finance. For Castoriadis, capitalism in this way incarnated a new social imaginary, predicated on the unlimited expansion of rational mastery of the modes of accumulation.

The autonomy of the subject and rational mastery thus found common ground in the concept of reason. With respect to the autonomy of the modern subject, reason was the possibility of freedom, the possibility of the individual to distinguish *ius* from *factum* and thereby to be able to decide the principles by which to live. But with respect to capitalism, reason was *Verstand* — "understanding" in the Kantian-Hegelian sense, or what Castoriadis called *ensemblistic-identitary logic*. This logic was embodied in quantification and led to the "fetishization of growth *per se*."[4] The idea of growth and development became a true idol of "modern times," and no other value — human, natural, or religious — could resist the process of maximization of profit implicit in capitalism's rational mastery as a "productive" application of reason. As Castoriadis wrote:

> Everything is called to the tribunal of (productive) Reason and must prove its right to exist on the basis of the criterion of the unlimited expansion of rational mastery. Through the unrestricted use of (pseudo-)rational ends, capitalism thus becomes a perpetual process of supposedly rational but essentially blind self-reinstitution of society.[5]

Reason understood as both the possibility of freedom and the dominion over capital thus became the common ground of autonomy and capitalism. Because of this it was also the battlefield of political, cultural, and social conflict within and against capitalism itself. This conflict was to reach its apogee in the 1960s when — for the last time — intellectual forces systematically challenged capitalism's political and cultural hegemony. Subsequently, with the advent of what Castoriadis defined as the third phase of the project of autonomy — the retreat into conformism — the very idea of political conflict was replaced by political agnosticism, meaning indifference toward the hegemony of capitalism. This indifference was seen by Castoriadis as the total disappearance of systematic criticism of capitalist rationality previously carried out by economists such as John Maynard Keynes and Piero Sraffa, and the passive acceptance of representative democracy. This political agnosticism and lack of theoretical thinking would become the fertile ground for schools of thought based on textual commentary and historical intepretation from "hermeneutics" to "deconstruction." Castoriadis states:

> What we have here is a collection of half-truths perverted into stratagems of evasion. The value of today's theory is that it mirrors prevailing trends. Its misery is that it simply rationalizes them through a highbrow apologetics of conformity and banality. Complacently mixed up with loose but fashionable talk about "pluralism" and "respect" for difference, for "the other," it ends up by glorifying eclecticism, covering up sterility and banality, and providing a generalized version of "anything goes."[6]

Against this background of political-intellectual agnosticism and stagnation over the last decade, and in the wake of events such as the G8 protests in Seattle in 1999 and Genoa in 2001, the question of autonomy from capitalism's ensemblistic-identitary logic has once again garnered attention. The global success of Michael Hardt and Antonio Negri's book Empire may be seen as the most visible sign of this change. For Hardt and Negri, capitalism has reached such a peak of development that it no longer needs any national legitimacy and affirms itself as a supranational, imperial entity. However, the same means that have led to its precipitous expansion — technological development, "immaterial" or post-Fordist labor, and the subjugating techniques of "biopower" — are also the features of a dispersed multitude that offers a form of political resistance to such an entity. If Hardt and Negri have projected the scenario of "class struggle" in the postmodern era, it is also true that their theoretical scheme of struggle — to fight and resist using the same means as one's oppressor — is not all that different from the one described by Castoriadis as the very core of the meaning of modernity.

For Castoriadis, reason was the ground of both the free subject and the rational mastery of capitalism; for Hardt and Negri, the infrastructure of Empire—including immaterial labor and biopower—constitutes both the structure of domination and the source of liberation. But while the project of autonomy for Castoriadis was a long-term, historical process that began with the invention of modern politics during the Renaissance, the origin of Negri and Hardt's project can be narrowed down to the concept of autonomy as elaborated in the vicissitudes of the Italian movement of intellectual activists in the 1970s known as Autonomia.

It is also true that the very tradition of political autonomy out of which Hardt and Negri's blockbuster arose, and of which it represents a clever *vulgata*—to the point of disarming its original source—has subtly lent itself to conformism with the "prevailing trends" of postmodern politics, from "pluralism" and "multiplicity" to the end of the working class. My argument, as will become clear in what follows, is that this conformism is a function of the fact that the very source of Hardt and Negri's "original" idea of autonomy, namely the Operaist, or Workerist, movement, was feared as too ambitious, too grand a narrative of modern politics, and therefore incompatible with—or, more precisely, indigestible by—the "postpolitical" and "postideological" aftermath of a defeated communism at the end of the 1980s. In this context, Italian Autonomia was presented to the English-speaking world in 1980 as a "creative, futuristic, neo-anarchistic, postideological, and nonrepresentative political movement."[7] It is this reading of autonomy that it is my intention to criticize, going beyond its claims to creativity and futurism and reconsidering its theoretical foundations.

What is understood today as Autonomia was an elite movement of intellectuals and activists that arose in Italy during the 1970s—more precisely, between 1969, the year of the *autunno caldo* (hot autumn), a season of intense workers' strikes following the 1968 student protests, and 1977, the year in which radical activists expressed their desire for political individualism by openly protesting and directing their fight against the official workers' organizations, seen as retrograde with respect to the political struggle. This position was a translation and

8

deformation of the main theses elaborated by a composite and controversial movement of activists and political thinkers known as Operaists that began in the 1960s,[8] which, as just suggested, should be seen as the progenitor of the Autonomia groups but also as something completely independent of them.[9]

The central thesis of Operaism, as formulated in its most radical theoretical fashion by the Roman philosopher and political thinker Mario Tronti, consisted of the argument that it was the workers' rebellious initiative against their work that caused capital to evolve, not the other way around. By looking at capitalism from this perspective, it appeared to be not an open-ended, natural evolution of "productive forces," but rather an exact measure of the power of the workers exercised *per via negativa*—in other words, of the ability of the workers, through their struggle against work, to force capital to keep evolving so as to disarm the ever-emerging possibilities of resistance. The movement took the name Operaism because the central element of this theory was the political subjectivity of the worker—the *operaio*—rather than the scientific objectivity of the production system. It should be made clear from the outset that although what became known as Autonomia had its origin in Operaism, the two are not interchangeable. The fundamental difference between them is that Operaism developed entirely within a communist perspective of politics and power, while Autonomia took a radically anti-communist stance, to the point of conflating itself with the many forms of postpolitical subjectivity that emerged within the crisis of political representation of the 1980s.

What I wish to argue here is that the most legitimate theoretical consequence of Operaism was Tronti's notion of the autonomy of the political: the discovery of an autonomous dimension of political power within the tradition of the working class.[10] Operaism conceived this project as a conscious "heresy" that made sense within the tradition of the working-class movement. For the Autonomia groups during the 1970s and 1980s, it became a way to translate the rising crisis of the workers as a relevant political subject through an imaginary escalation of workers' power. In this situation, in which, as Tronti said, "the red sky of the working class's sunset was misunderstood as the red sky of the dawn,"[11] the main target of Autonomia and the site of

9

its struggle became not so much the fight against capitalism as a subtle attack on the institutions of the Left as the emblematic elements of social and cultural retardation within the highly advanced trajectory of capitalism. This is why the theoretical contribution of Autonomia, which was less original in its conception (since this was inherited from Operaism), turned out to be so creative. This creativity served to elevate the subjects of the political struggle culturally, but it often devolved into mystification. As part of this process of cultural elevation, social semantics and the invention of new terms played an important role. In the Autonomist lexicon, the industrial mass worker of the 1960s became the "social worker" of the 1970s; finally, in the 1990s and 2000s, he turned into the "multitude." Under such transformations, capitalism appeared bit by bit to abandon its paternalistic intentions to be a state plan on the model of the post–World War II welfare state and to take on the trappings of a more sophisticated form of command, the high-tech and extra-state Empire. Yet while the Autonomists succeeded—following Operaism's *modus operandi* of the working class—in establishing a convincing and fascinating narrative to explain why capitalism had changed and evolved into its present form, it was more difficult for them to explain the reasons the subject struggling against the Empire of capitalism had moved, and was continuing to move, forward. If, according to Negri and Hardt, the multitude's impetus for emancipation was a product of the very biopowers that constituted the deep infrastructure of Empire, what kind of *telos* constituted the autonomy of this subject from the logic of the power that subjugated it?

The answer that the Autonomists, and more recently Negri and Hardt, proposed to this question often coincided with the imperative of production seen through (or concealed by) suggestive concepts, at times romantic, at times futuristic, such as their insistent science of desire. This was the trigger for individual *cupiditas* unrestricted by any (political) limitations and the manipulation of human life seen as a victory over traditional distinctions between human and animal, human and machine. But is it not in this *modus vivendi* of the human subject that capitalism currently fully invests, transforming human labor into its most efficient productive force? Does not the reproduction of capital occur in our minds as a psychological process of "objectification" of desire, individualism, and subjectivity itself? In this sense, the argument of the Autonomists still depended on the logic of capitalism, which in its deepest essence is the stimulus for the unlimited desire of production supported by the mastery of technological development as a way to create and re-create the conditions of its own reproduction. Autonomy was thus *de facto* transformed by the Autonomists into its opposite: heteronomy. The workers in turn—the collective subject exploited by capitalism through its transformation into paid labor and thereby expropriated not simply of its own product but of its prerogatives over production (that is, the decision whether to produce)—became the fancy "multitude."

It is within this context of political opportunism that the legacy of Autonomia in the 1970s has recently been celebrated, while the project of autonomy prior to the 1970s has been overlooked. The multitude became a subject that was seen as existing in a state of pseudo-anarchic hypercreativity rather than as making political decisions to limit, frame, and form the need for production (and thereby the conditions of consumption). Thus, if the project of autonomy in its original meaning of a grand and radical reconstruction of the political subject—one that not only resisted capitalism but demanded power over it—could not avoid the collapse of Communism, in the 1970s and especially the 1980s it became a postpolitical practice. Autonomy became a way neither to master nor to resist capitalism but instead to transform it by means of a very sophisticated hermeneutics of its cultural effects, and within the highly progressive perspective of the development of forces that were supposed to be its antagonist.

Against this scenario, it is my aim in the following pages to reopen the question of the project of autonomy, challenging not simply its contemporary cultural status and revival, but its historical interpretation. Instead of privileging the Autonomia movement of the 1970s, I shall consider the development of this project as it took form in Italy during the 1960s. My shift in focus is motivated not just by the desire to go back to the formative period of Italian autonomy in order to demystify the current

11

interpretation and success of Autonomia as it emerged the 1970s, but also to attempt to extract from that preceding history what is still valid today. A shift from the celebrated Autonomia of the 1970s to its premises in the 1960s is crucial in order to understand what was really at stake in this project. My argument is that for Operaism, and for a number of Italian movements or groups that formed around the same time, the possibility of autonomy was not a generic claim of autonomy *from*, but rather a more audacious and radical claim of autonomy *for*. This *autonomy for* consisted of a bid by the workers to construct a source of power alternative to the one established and maintained by capitalism.

My interpretation of autonomy within the domain of politics will be complemented by a survey of the idea of autonomy as it took form in other domains as well. In this context, I shall analyze the theoretical vicissitudes of the fundamental conception of *autonomia* that emerged and evolved in Italian architectural theories and debates of the 1960s but that, like its political version, has tended to be popularized more as a product of the 1970s. Anglo-Saxon architectural culture associates "autonomous architecture" with a period of recent architectural history in which the autonomy of architectural form from political, social, and commercial significations was "discovered." This particular reading emerged at a moment of increasing commercialization of architecture as a professional practice and, in Europe, coincided with the decadence of public and state initiatives as a primary application of architecture and urban design. In this context, the concept of autonomy in architecture was immediately translated as a strategic retreat, a refusal to reform the existing world. Within this context radically different personalities like Aldo Rossi and Manfredo Tafuri in Italy and Peter Eisenman and Colin Rowe in the United States were grouped together by virtue of their common critical point of view toward the exhaustion of the reformist apparatus of the Modern Movement in the context of post–World War II architectural culture.

There is no doubt that this shared perspective was important and vital for the development of a critical architectural theory in the 1970s. However, the interpretation of the work of Rossi and Tafuri, especially, suffered from significant misunderstandings.

These misunderstandings were not only a result of the fact that their respective work was generally understood, and not only abroad but also in Italy, as sharing a common position; in fact, the Milanese architect and the Roman historian held different, if not radically opposite, points of view on architecture and its politics. Misunderstandings also occurred with the removal of Rossi's idea of an autonomous architecture from its political, social, and historical context. For Rossi, autonomy entailed a refusal not of the reality of the emerging postindustrial city, but of the empirical interpretation of that reality and of the naive embrace of techno-utopian visions of the contemporary world. As I shall argue later, for Rossi the possibility of autonomy occurred as a possibility of theory: of the reconstruction of the political, social, and cultural significations of urban phenomena divorced from any technocratic determinism.

In this sense, Rossi's idea of autonomy in architecture and urbanism reveals interesting similarities to the one elaborated by Tronti in politics. In the face of capitalism's total absorption of the technological rationality of planning, Rossi sought to privilege architecture as the most vital field for the theoretical reinvention of the city—architecture, that is, without the mediation of planning. As Rossi began to elaborate this position in the early 1960s while working as an architect and contributing to the magazine Casabella continuità, a group of young architects, most of them teaching at the Istituto Universitario di Archittetura di Venezia (IUAV), and all with very close ties to the Communist Party, informally gathered around him. With Rossi teaching at the IUAV from 1963 to 1965 as assistant to Carlo Aymonino, chair of the newly established "Organizational Characteristics of Buildings" program, this group was consolidated, and with encouragement from Giuseppe Samonà, the director of the school, it soon became recognizable as the nucleus of the "Scuola di Venezia."[12]

Much like Operaism, whose identity was absorbed by its later development as Autonomia, this original nucleus—which from now on I will call the "Venice Group," and which further developed in the 1970s at the IUAV, without Rossi, as the "Gruppo Architettura"[13]—was subsequently overshadowed in the international reception of Italian architecture by both

5

13

the myth of a different "school of Venice" dominated by Tafuri (who joined the IUAV only in 1968 and founded the "Istituto di Storia" there) and the myth of the "Tendenza," the group of architects who gathered around Rossi some time after the publication of L'architettura della città (The architecture of the city), which appeared in 1966 after Rossi had become a professor at the Politecnico in Milan. Rossi taught in Milan until 1971, and then, after his expulsion for supporting student occupations and encouraging collective diplomas, at the Eidgenössische Technische Hochschule (ETH) in Zurich in the mid 1970s.

Before all of this, however, there was the Venice Group, a small, informal community of architects who set a style of pedagogy that immediately gained recognition for its preference for a theory of architecture and the city over professional practice. This attitude, which was also a reaction to the long dominance at the IUAV of such craft-oriented professionals as Carlo Scarpa, manifested itself in the habit of preparing classes and lectures based on theoretical writings that were then discussed among the participants in the group. A very similar attitude, although in a completely different context and with different political attitudes, as we shall see, also characterized the formation of Archizoom and Superstudio in Florence a few years later.[14] If Rossi and the Venice Group were clearly influenced by the politics of the Communist Party, the Florentine groups were influenced more by the political and ideological themes of Operaism and its revolt against institutional organizations. Yet like the Venice Group, their formation was marked by a strong preference for theoretical research and speculation over professional practice.

As I aim to demonstrate, these two types of autonomy projects—one applied to politics, one applied to the city—were not about the destruction of capitalist culture and bourgeois history *per se* but, on the contrary, their deep analysis and instrumental use. Autonomy was not the creation of politics and poetics *ex nihilo* but rather an audacious effort to appropriate the political realm in order to construct an alternative to capitalist domination.

Autonomy and the Left

A very important task for the specifically political groups in Italy during the 1960s was to reconstruct, first, a rigorous theoretical approach from within the working-class movement. It was as a product of this theoretical anxiety that the question of autonomy first emerged. What was debated was the workers' autonomy not only from capitalism, but also from those anticapitalist organizations that, because of the institutional role they assumed within the bourgeois-democratic state, had become *de facto* an essential political and social conduit for the workers' integration within the capitalist process.

This emerging debate found its early theoretical formulation in both France and Italy between the early 1950s and the early 1960s in the pages of two fundamental political journals: the Paris-based Socialisme ou barbarie (Socialism or barbarism, 1948–65), founded and led by Cornelius Castoriadis and Claude Lefort; and the Turinese-Roman Quaderni rossi (Red notebooks, 1961–65), founded by the political thinker Raniero Panzieri. It was around the latter that the group of political activists and intellectuals later to be called the Operaists took form.[15] Both of these journals put forward a demand for a renewal of working-class analysis and politics distinct from that of the Communist Party establishment. This demand may be seen as an outcome of the watershed events in the history of the European Left that took place in 1956: the Twentieth Party Congress held in Moscow in February, where Nikita Khrushchev admitted and criticized the political excesses of Stalin; and the Red Army's bloody suppression of the revolution in Hungary. Together these two events, combined with the conformism that Left-oriented trade unions and party organizations in Western Europe were forced to embrace in order to survive institutionally within the geopolitics of the Cold War, pushed many activists and intellectuals to reinvent the politics of the workers' movement.

This reinvention often ran directly counter to the policies of the liberal state in which the official organizations of the Left had grown up. But while for those who gravitated toward Socialisme ou barbarie this position led to open criticism and rejection not just of Stalin's legacy but also of Lenin's Bolshevik revolution, those gathering around Quaderni rossi opted for a different position, more risky and theoretically daring: rather than reject the Marxist-Leninist legacy, they embraced it *tout court,* confronting the collapse of Stalinism and the conformism of the traditional workers' organizations from the contemporary perspective of liberal democracy as imposed by the capitalist states in Europe after World War II. In other words, instead of abandoning communism in the name of the liberties offered by liberalism, the Italian activists opted for a more analytically rigorous, politically radical, and intellectually sophisticated reading of communism's original sources. According to many of these thinkers, the problem of socialism was not so much that Soviet Russia had transformed the revolution into a state dictatorship, but the fact that the very idea of revolution had been replaced by a peaceful coexistence between the workers and liberal institutions that was underwritten by capitalism. In order to reestablish a revolutionary perspective, the Operaists assumed the primary necessity of refounding an operative workers' autonomy, and this took the form of a new theoretical paradigm, which they called "the workers' point of view." This paradigm consisted of conceptualizing the struggle between the working class and capitalism not from the standpoint of capitalist development, but from that of the working-class struggle.

In order to understand this paradigm correctly, it is important to clarify immediately what we mean by working class besides its well-known historical iconography of the blue collar. To speak of the working class is to speak of "living labor," the collectivity of producers of material and immaterial goods who receive wages in exchange for their work. This work product, which is immediately expropriated by the capitalist division of labor, is put into circulation in the form of commodities. According to orthodox Marxism, industrial production contains its own logic, which leads to the progressive development of society; the exploitation of the worker occurs only in the context of the anarchic system of circulation and distribution, which represents the source of capitalism's profit and advantage over the workers. Operaism opposed this orthodox belief in the contradiction between production, on the one hand, and circulation and distribution, on the other. For the Operaists, the system of production itself—through the continuity of its technological development and the sophistication and innovation of its division of labor—was the source of capitalism's power over the working class. It was for this reason that the Operaists shifted their attention from an analysis of capitalism understood through its effects of circulation, distribution, and consumption toward a structural and global analysis of capitalism in terms of its deepest source of power: the power over production. For the Operaists, the project of autonomy had to begin at this level in order to become politically effective, and it had, moreover, to coincide not with a reform of the means of production but with a demand for political power over them.

As a result, Operaism no longer performed its analysis of capitalism at the level of the presumed rationality of the system but rather at the level of the producer's conflictual position as this was embodied by the political, and not simply social, existence of the workers organized as a class. The existence of the working class was seen as a projective struggle, a struggle that, in opposing capitalism, defined itself as a culturally and politically innovative and creative collective subject. To accomplish this, the Operaists developed two approaches. The first was research from within the modes of spontaneous working-class organization, which the Operaists called *conricerca:* research undertaken from the working-class point of view, and as such opposed to bourgeois methods of social inquiry and evaluation. The second was a theoretical formulation concerning the ways this subject could constitute itself beyond spontaneous and passive forms of resistance.

The context in which this redefinition of the working class took place was the transition from a form of capitalism based on traditional types of competition to what the Operaists called *neocapitalism,* a more organized and diffuse form of capitalism, in which oligarchic and monopolistic types of control were more visible. The key phrase in this transition was *economic planning.* What was taking place in Italy and throughout Europe in the 1960s was what had occurred in the United States in the 1930s: the system of production was becoming more efficiently organized. This meant a more generalized and extensive dissemination of industrial production beyond the factory to the whole of society.

In the 1960s, neocapitalism became the organic link between the capitalist system of accumulation and the programs of the welfare state. If traditional competitive capitalism had focused in a rudimentary way on the accumulation of profits by taking for granted the social conditions of its labor force, neocapitalism provided more sophisticated types of social assistance for workers, going beyond the working hours. As Adolf Berle has written, the neocapitalist enterprise focuses on the wealth of its labor force because this also means the wealth of its consumers, which means the wealth of society as a whole.[16] Raniero Panzieri would add:

> The factory is busy not simply with production of material goods, but with society at large. This is because in order to maintain, defend, and develop its power, the factory must plan itself in an incessant process of integration with the whole social body. Thus the tendency to social planning is intrinsic to the new modes of production of the neocapitalist factory.[17]

It is for this reason that it is important not to confine our view of the autonomy project to the traditional iconography and rather narrow thinking of the groups of the 1970s, but instead to open our analysis of their hypotheses concerning the working class to more general conditions of political work and intellectual militancy. These not only emerged in the formulations of the Operaists, but also took shape within a broader spectrum of autonomy projects in Italy that defined themselves *within* but also *against* capitalism. In this context of a renewed theoretical approach to the analysis of the city and its politics, the technocratic "humanism" of the welfare state and its cultural and built representations were ferociously attacked.

Autonomy and the Intellectuals

A crucial consequence of neocapitalism in its tendency to transform the entire social spectrum into a productive system is the radical transformation of intellectual work. If intellectuals like Italo Calvino and Pier Paolo Pasolini accepted or, conversely, criticized the new forms of consumerist society, taking for granted their own position vis-à-vis the social relationships imposed by the new system of production, others like the poet Franco Fortini went beyond the myth of cultural consumption in order to question the role of intellectuals as producers of culture, and eventually of an autonomous political position within capitalism.[18] It was within the perspective of the economic integration of culture within the new organization of labor that Fortini conceived the figure of the intellectual no longer as a vocation but—to put it in Max Weber's words—a "profession." In light of this new professional dimension of intellectual work, an entire generation of intellectuals and theorists who were in their thirties in the 1960s began to see aesthetic detachment as a nonviable conception of autonomy. On the contrary, they considered the only path to autonomy to be a rigorous stance with respect to political positioning and political decision within society's new forms and relations of production. "Against from within" became a way to refuse capitalist power structures through rigorous knowledge of how these structures manifested themselves in relation to questions of political decision, cultural work, and poetic experience.

This new political urgency gave form to a particular way of organizing intellectual and political militancy that coalesced in the idea of the group. Beyond the intellectual and existential solidarity that this type of social association inevitably entails, the idea of the group was also understood in terms of the dichotomy of friend/enemy,[19] which was a way of combating both the false illusion of the impartiality of culture and the established cultural politics of party organizations and official political institutions. Groups of intellectuals such as Gruppo '63 in literature and the cadre who gathered about Aldo Rossi in architecture formed around the idea of a new political subject and immediately tested this idea as an act of *poiesis*. Their collectively established poetics were explicitly conceived as a confrontational device with respect to the background from which they claimed political and cultural autonomy. If Antonio Gramsci had theorized the role of the intellectual as an organic figure within the hegemonic context of the Communist Party organization, the groups of the 1960s saw themselves in relation to the new forms of diffuse capitalism as the manifestation of

19

a will to separate from, to oppose, the gradual integration of culture with the political forms of liberal democracy. Moreover, the members of these groups saw their work no longer as individual contributions to be offered to a larger society of individuals, but on the contrary as a collective experience that would manifest itself, in the revolutionary spirit of secession, in the form of a politically one-sided communality. It is interesting to recall a letter that the poet Fortini wrote to Pier Giorgio Bellocchio, the founder of Quaderni piacentini, one of the most important political and cultural journals of the 1960s:

> To the inevitable constitution within society of psycho-social communities and moral-cultural castes, the perspective of the new communism must oppose the possibility both of the community as a place of an ethically rich life and of political action as a verification of the richness of that life. Let the new groups govern themselves through the unwritten law of a common finality and conception of the world. These groups are neither pressure groups nor political lobbies (in the "functional," and therefore "liberal," sense of the term)—a role accepted in Italy even by the official Marxist parties. These groups should develop on whatever basis (of common profession, union membership, friendship, or generation) a responsible political consciousness—a *vision du monde.* Formations of this type have always occurred in the course of history; they have always defined the premises of political formations, which, in turn, have evolved as hegemonic forces. By their initial and radical refusal of the historical "reality" that surrounds them, they resemble certain aristocratic societies, a type with which the ancient and modern history of the West is replete. But by their commitment to change reality they avoid the pride of caste and of eventual degeneration.[20]

The idea of the group as a social aristocracy should not be seen as contradicting the idea of intellectual work as a profession. Here the ideal of social aristocracy means the affirmation of a position that refuses the open-ended forms of cultural debate typical of a liberal society. Against pluralism, the group affirms the superiority and irreducibility of the position it represents, not by asserting the presumed scientific truth of its own analysis, but by offering the possibility of transforming its position into a critical weapon in the service of the part of society it wishes to support.[21]

In the following pages I shall reconstruct the project of

autonomy not so much in terms of political and architectural groups as such, however, as of their theoretical positions. I shall focus on Raniero Panzieri, Mario Tronti, Aldo Rossi and Archizoom. Panzieri and Tronti were the most important figures associated with the development of Operaism. Rossi and Archizoom represented two opposing schools of thought—those that in the 1970s would be popularized as, respectively, the Tendenza and Radical Architecture. What these four intellectuals and the groups of which they were a part had in common was the fact that they were responsible for theorizing—at least during their most formative period—a politics alternative to the one imposed by capitalist reality. The challenge formulated by each of the four protagonists will be analyzed in its theoretical premises. What I propose is to compose their voices and their various projects of autonomy into an approach that may potentially be understood as a single project. I shall articulate this composition in five parts: the attempt to produce a rigorous analysis of capitalism (Panzieri); the theory of workers' political power (Tronti); the definition of the autonomy of the political (Tronti and Massimo Cacciari); the political conceptualization of the city and its architecture (Rossi); and finally, the proposal of a theory of the capitalist metropolis as a precondition for workers' autonomy (Branzi). I intend this five-part composition as an initial contribution to a historical reconstruction of the intense season of political and poetical imagination that unfolded in Italy over the course of the 1960s.

Panzieri: Capitalism and Technological Innovation
Are One and the Same

A fundamental point of departure for the project of autonomy in Italy was Raniero Panzieri's attack on the "objectivist" and "economist" ideology implicit in the Marxist theory of the development of the capitalist forces of production. Formed as a political activist in the Italian Socialist Party (PSI) and as an innovative interpreter and translator into Italian of Marx's writings, Panzieri did not live to see the development of his seminal ideas, dying prematurely in 1965 at the age of forty-three.

Indisputably, however, his role was essential in forming a critique of production that anticipates today's discussions of biopower and of capitalism's extension of its dominion through technological development. Panzieri agreed with the urgency felt by the unions and the workers' movement in general to focus attention on the new forms of industrial development. However, in light of the collapse of so-called realized communism within the Soviet bloc, and of his party's enthusiasm for technological development seen as a way to rationalize the apparent anarchy of capitalism, he soon realized that the attention to technological development as a pure form, idealized and devoid of concrete relationships with the factors of power within the capitalist organization of society, was a distraction. In an innovative and provocative essay published in the first issue of Quaderni rossi titled "Sull'uso delle macchine nel neo-capitalismo" (On the neocapitalist use of machinery),[22] he wrote:

> It has not even been suspected that capitalism might use the new "technical bases" offered by the passage from its preceding stages to that of full-scale mechanization (and automation) in order to perpetuate and consolidate the authoritarian structure of factory organization: indeed, the entire process of industrialization has been represented as being dominated by a "technological destiny" that leads to the liberation of man from the "limitations imposed on him by the environment and by his physical capabilities." "Administrative rationalization" and the enormous growth of external organizational functions are alike viewed in a "technical" or "pure" form. The relationship between these developments and the processes and contradictions of contemporary capitalism (its quest for ever more complex means to accomplish and impose its plans) and the concrete historical reality in which the working-class movement finds itself living and fighting (the daily "capitalist use" of machinery and organization)—all these are ignored in favor of a techno-romantic image.[23]

According to Panzieri, orthodox Marxism had falsely separated the process of the production of goods from the process of their valuation. The former process was "naturalized"; it was very optimistically and trustingly envisioned as the "development of the forces of production." The production of value was seen, on the other hand, as a function of capitalism's tendency toward accumulation. It was for this reason that orthodox Marxism—and indeed most Marxian theories and philosophies—tended to overlook the moment of production and address its criticism to the modes of circulation, distribution, and consumption. This led it to propose the possibility of an "automatic" reversal of the use of the products of workers' labor through the socialist appropriation of the process of production. It was thus on the presumed neutral ground of technology that Marxist objectivism and neocapitalism met. The historical context in which this encounter took place was the new industrial landscape of the 1960s, characterized by the increasing mass consumption of goods and the expansion of the white-collar and service sectors, rendering an image of European society as affluent and opulent. It was in this context that the official Communist Party organizations saw political conflict as an obsolete means of emancipation, incompatible with the increasing rationality of the new phase of capitalism.

Against this enthusiasm, Panzieri opposed the view that it was the presumed, or pseudo-rational, mastery of the means of production that was the core of capitalism's despotic political power. "Capitalist planning presupposes the planning of living labor," Panzieri writes, "and the more it strives to present itself as a closed, perfectly rational system of rules, the more it is abstract and partial, ready to be utilized solely in a hierarchical type of organization."[24] In the face of this capitalist "rationality," there could be no weapon other than the political subjectivity of the workers—that is, nothing except a bid for power by those who produced and therefore demanded "not rationality, but control; not technical programming, but a plan to empower the associated producers."[25]

But what theoretical premises brought Panzieri to reevaluate the subjectivity of the workers against—but from within—their very use of the capitalist machinery? By revising the tradition of Marxism, Panzieri discovered a possibility of workers' autonomy within a more rigorous reading of Marx, especially those parts of Das Kapital in which Marx theorized how the working class depended for its very existence on a process of demystification of bourgeois capitalist ideology. He supported Marx's insight that cooperation among the workers was the simplest representation of collective work, but more important, it was

23

also the fundamental form of capitalist production. Capitalism presupposed the freedom of the individual worker to sell his own labor. The problem was that this freedom existed only when the worker entered individually into a relationship with capitalism. As Marx affirmed, the cooperation of the workers—that is, their transformation from free individuals to a society of workers—always occurred under capitalist domination since capitalism's vested interest was to organize the labor force for maximum productivity. In this way, the workers' social cooperation was appropriated by capitalism for free at the very inception of the production cycle. The productive social force of labor, the organized cooperation that made a mass of workers productive, was thus repossessed by capitalism as something natural: as an "immanent force of production," as Marx put it. Through the progress of technology, the capitalist organization of production underwent an evolution from a system of coercion to a system of persuasion, becoming a form of work that was ever more sophisticated and devoid of connotations that betrayed its exploitative character.

By considering this evolutionary aspect of the conditions of capitalist work, Panzieri overturned Marx and Engels's argument in the Communist Manifesto concerning capitalism's loss of attraction for the worker once his job became organized under a strict and efficient division of labor. To Marx and Engels's assertion that labor would lose its attraction for individual workers as they increasingly became an appendage of the machine, Panzieri opposed the contemporary scenario of incessant technological evolution in the direction of full automation of machinery and information as creating greater attraction for workers. He wrote:

In the use of "informational" technologies to manipulate working-class attitudes, capitalism has incalculably vast margins for acquiescence (or rather, "stabilization"). It is impossible to define the limit beyond which "information" concerning the overall productive processes ceases to be a stabilizing factor for capitalist power. What is certain is that information technologies tend, in the more complex situation of the contemporary capitalist enterprise, to restore that "charm" (satisfaction) of work of which the Communist Manifesto once spoke.[26]

Thus, for Panzieri, the expanding wealth and social well-being of the workers was a factor in their political dependency on capitalism:

> The introduction of newer machines, the stimulus to research, to new scientific discoveries and their application within an unending process of technological development—these are the essence of capitalist accumulation. Capitalist accumulation consists of an overwhelming wave of new technologies as a means of human domination of nature. That is precisely why it is the factor of innovation in the process of accumulation that produces surplus.[27]

The extraction of this surplus, and thus of profit, was therefore the basic impetus for capitalist innovation. Innovation became profit not only when it permitted a reduction in the size of the labor force but also when its increasing technical sophistication, and its totalizing distribution of this sophistication, made it impossible to imagine any other perspective beyond its own advancing means of production. According to Panzieri, in order to maintain this dynamic state, capitalism had to establish its continuity through abrupt leaps forward. These convulsive technological leaps were then projected by capitalism into the world in two ways: on the level of production, as an amelioration of the conditions of labor; and on the level of consumption, as improvements in the product.

It was through a critique of this "apologetic" character within the development of capitalism's forces of production that Panzieri defined the possibility of the workers' autonomy from capitalism. Focusing his attention on the ideological conditions under which, by means of its incessant technological innovations, capitalism continuously produced new jobs, new skills, and new expertise, he elaborated how, within the process of development of the forces of production, capitalism also tended to disqualify traditional products of labor (even when these were still necessary). In constantly launching new products, some of which were truly innovative but others of which were little more than mere semantic inventions, capitalism aimed, by seizing the cultural, social, and scientific consequences of its technological innovations, to integrate labor as much as possible into its political regime. A crucial example of this integrative capacity for Panzieri was the Olivetti factory in Ivrea. Panzieri viewed Olivetti as bringing together innovation, social welfare, and culture. Directed by Adriano Olivetti, an "enlightened" entrepreneur and reformer, the Olivetti factory was intended to be a model community of workers, a center of "humanistic" production, focused not just on the development of information technology but on its social and cultural consequences. From the 1930s on, Olivetti acted as a patron of modern architecture, seen by him as a progressive language in which to construct a space of production in keeping with his objectives, by commissioning the company's most important buildings and facilities of Italian architects like Luigi Figini and Gino Pollini, and Ignazio Gardella.[28] In order to maintain this spirit, Olivetti also involved as "employees" intellectuals such as Franco Fortini and the left-wing writer Paolo Volponi.

Panzieri, however, saw the Olivetti model as the culmination of advanced capitalist ideology, with culture itself becoming an essential moment of production. "Look at Olivetti," Panzieri wrote polemically, "it is a feudal court with this vicious facade of intellectuals working on programs and research that are nothing but a masquerade of capitalism's will to integrate the whole of society."[29] Even worse for Panzieri was the sociological analysis of work practiced by reformist bourgeois intellectuals, who portrayed the neocapitalist rationalization of the means of production and the subsequent evolution of labor as "humanistic" advances. These intellectuals saw in the company's deployment of its technological resources the individual's positive reappropriation of the content of his labor and his transformation from a worker into a technician and consumer.

From Panzieri's standpoint, the workers' control of the technological means of production could hardly be seen in itself as an alternative to alienation. In his view, it was crucial for the workers to control those means politically, by taking charge of the labor process that these "reforms" and "innovations" tended to establish. It was on this point that Panzieri entered into strong polemic with the French sociologist Georges Friedmann, whose important book Où va le travail humain? (Whither human work?)—a book translated into Italian by the publishing house of Olivetti—naively used Marx's theses concerning the evolution of work to interpret automation as signifying an increasing ability of the individual to control his own labor psychically and physically.

Panzieri was critical not simply of the apologetic voices defending the transformation of labor by means of technological development, however, but also of those who opposed to this same development a completely pessimistic outlook, such as Theodor W. Adorno. Panzieri admired both Adorno's intransigent position with respect to any forms of affirmation of the new forms of technological development and, especially, his critique of how those forms ended up producing totally distorted cultural representations of themselves. In an intervention at the first congress of the Operaists, he quoted the following words from Adorno's Minima Moralia:

What the philosophers once knew as life has become the sphere of private existence and now of mere consumption, dragged along as an appendage of the process of material production, without autonomy or substance of its own. He who wishes to know the truth about life in its immediacy must scrutinize its estranged form, the objective powers that determine individual existence even in its most hidden recesses.[30]

But Panzieri also offered a qualification of Adorno's position:

This passage from Adorno is very interesting and it appears to us correct. But then, although he is addressing objective forces, his critique gets stuck on the level of consumption, which is the most visible layer of alienation. But we know that consumption in itself is just a half-truth of the overall process.[31]

If for Adorno the individual's protest against the system could only be addressed at the level of consumption, then, according to Panzieri, he and critics like him had failed to make an accurate analysis of production, its social mechanisms, and its political organization. Panzieri emphasized Adorno's inability to extend his acute discourse on aesthetics—Panzieri was also a great admirer of Adorno's writings on music—beyond the consequences of capitalism to the political control of capitalist production. For Panzieri, the great limitation of philosophers like Adorno was that they completely missed the increasing proletarianization of the rest of society—that is, of the white-collar and service sector, which they considered only in terms of its alienated forms of middle-class consumption. It was not by chance that Adorno, as Panzieri noted, had rhetorically asked: "The sociologists are confronted with a ferociously comic question: where is the proletariat?"

It was precisely the effort to give a clear and demystifying political, and not sociological, answer to this question on which the whole Operaist project of autonomy rested. For Panzieri, in the context of capitalism's increasingly greater economic integration of society, autonomy meant demystification of technological development and the taking of control of this development by the workers *per via politica.* This implied the need to understand production and consumption as one indissoluble process. In his essay "Plusvalore e planificazione" (Surplus value and planning), Panzieri supported this insight with a critique of the ideological representation of the mechanisms of capitalist production.[32] He began by recalling Lenin's reaffirmation that the object of political economy was the production not of material goods but of the social relations created by the relations of production. Panzieri noted, however, that Lenin himself had failed to see the contributing role of technology and its increasingly sophisticated knowledge in forging those relations.

What, then, was the fundamental role of machinery in the factory? For Panzieri, it was to appropriate what at the end of the process constituted the real surplus of capitalist production: workers' cooperation. The labor force, initially a mass of individuals, became, once it transformed into a cooperative group, a productive force that capitalism could make use of for free. As Panzieri writes, "In its capitalist form, cooperation is the fundamental law of surplus."[33] He goes on to say, referring to Marx, that for this reason the bonds among workers are ultimately inimical to their own interests because they faciliate capitalism's economic plans—that is, because they are socially authorized by the capitalist system. As such, workers are organized by a political force that exists outside of them and for purposes imposed on them.

Against this scenario, Panzieri proposed what he called

"workers' control" as the ultimate act of subversion of the capitalist system by the workers: their capacity not to direct their pressure at reform of the system on the social level, but to take political power over it democratically. As he writes in "Sul controllo operaio" (On workers' control):

> [T]he political battle of the workers' movement cannot be reduced to the space of the factory, but must be fought at all levels of society. However, the fundamental place of this battle is the factory in its character as a mode of production; it is here that the worker must oppose the social conditions of production with his struggle. The problem of workers' control is the call for antagonism at the level of the centers of production.[34]

In spite of the lucidity of this analysis, Panzieri would not be able to go beyond his ambiguous proposal for the workers to take control of society through democratic means. The Quaderni rossi position would remain at the level of an analytical approach to the problem of the working class. The questions that would increasingly arise among the Operaists in the aftermath of Panzieri's analysis were the following: What political conclusion could be projected out of his analysis in order to overturn the status quo imposed by the productive forces of capitalism? What kind of approach to the status quo could be theorized so as to transform the working-class point of view into a viable political position concerning "workers' control"?

A concrete answer to these questions was implicitly given by the so-called events of Piazza Statuto in Turin, which took place in 1962. Turin—the Detroit of Italy—possessed in the 1950s and 1960s the most advanced forms of industrial production by virtue of the presence there of FIAT, the leading Italian automobile industry. In the late 1950s and early 1960s the city became a center of massive immigration from the south of the country, which contributed dramatically to changing the features of its working class. No longer was the "skilled worker," with his pride as a producer and his dependence on established unions, the protagonist of Italian labor. Owing to the immense quantitative leap in industrial production as an effect of the abundant new supply of workers, what emerged in Italy's industrial north, and especially in Turin, was an entirely different kind of proletariat.

It was much more alienated and thus rebellious against, if not indifferent toward, work. The new workers did not just dislike their jobs, they hated them. Their dependence on the factory was purely opportunistic and devoid of traditional workers' ethics and responsibility toward production.

In July 1962, the workers represented by the so-called yellow union, UIL, the reformist wing within the syndicate, signed a renewal of contract separately from the "red unions," the unions representing the more leftist workers. One of the red unions, CGIL, organized a demonstration that was supposed to march from the FIAT factory toward the seat of the UIL. Although the demonstration was intended by the union leaders to be peaceful, some of the workers provoked an intense guerrilla fight against the UIL, which then spread throughout the city. The struggle was massive and lasted several days. What was most impressive and shocking for many left-wing activists, however, was that for the first time the workers were openly contesting the political boundaries set by the unions. The workers were now directing their protest against the unions themselves, seen as an integral part of the system.

The Piazza Statuto protest revealed to the Operaists better than any sociological analysis the features of the new political subject: the mass worker. This subject was no longer a passive and well-organized leftist militant proud of his condition as a worker-producer and defined ideologically by the democratic politics of the official organizations of the workers' movement. Instead, he was much more cynical about his work, and thus—here was the paradox—potentially much more effective in his struggle against the repressive and paternalistic policies of the factory. What was especially notable was that the workers' hatred of their work was a direct result of capitalism's advance toward a more sophisticated system of production. Celebrated by the Operaists as the emergence of a *rude razza pagana* (rude pagan race), the new mass worker was seen as inaugurating the possibility of a revolutionary new perspective on the working-class movement at the most advanced levels of capitalist social organization.

At the same time, it was in offering an answer to the scenario of which Piazza Statuto was the most shocking symptom that the group around Panzieri would break into two parts. Panzieri himself was very skeptical about how much importance to attribute to the Turin events, and he saw the mass workers' anarchic forms of protest as politically nihilistic. The intellectuals in the group gathered around Mario Tronti, however, saw in the protests the possibility to move from a purely analytical theory of the working class to a revolutionary practice. But the difference of position between Panzieri and Tronti was even more subtle and fundamental. For Panzieri, the autonomy of the workers had to be built from below through an intensification of the social analysis of their condition and a proposal to organize them democratically. For Tronti, the only way to organize the workers' reaction was through direct struggle. Autonomy for Tronti, who unlike the rest of the Operaists was still a member of the Communist Party, thus meant the possibility of seeing the whole of society as a struggle of one part of society against another part, of workers against capital.

Tronti: Society Is a Factory

The group aligned with Mario Tronti at the beginning of 1964 included, among others, the literary historian Alberto Asor Rosa, the political activist Rita di Leo, the young assistant professor of philosophy at the University of Padua Antonio Negri, the historians Umberto Coldagelli and Gaspare De Caro, and the young philosophy student and activist Massimo Cacciari. The monthly journal they founded, Classe operaia (Working class), was—at least at the beginning—less essayistic than Quaderni rossi and more focused on political intervention. From the start, Tronti had played an important role in Quaderni rossi, publishing three fundamental essays in it that distinguished his position from Panzieri's. In contrast to the latter's critique of technological development, Tronti affirmed in his essay "Il piano del capitale" (The plan of capital) that while the development of capitalism was responsible for the improved treatment of the working class, it was, in fact, the pressure of the labor force that triggered capitalism's response and determined the level of its development, not vice versa.[35] In other words, the trigger of capitalist development was capitalism's need to organize itself in response to the working class. Capitalism thus implicitly recognized the strategic centrality of the working class, which, by virtue of being paid labor, constituted its foundation. The more capitalism developed, Tronti suggested, the more it had to keep in mind that the working class was a constant threat to it; at any moment this class could find a way to subvert the system simply by being a developmental trigger. Following Lenin, Tronti wrote:

> [T]he idea of searching for the salvation of the workers everywhere except in the further development of capitalism is a reactionary idea. The working class suffers more the insufficiencies of capitalist development than capitalism itself. The bourgeois revolution offers great advantages to the proletariat; it is, in a certain sense, much more useful to the proletariat than to the bourgeoisie itself.[36]

This position constituted a total reversal of Panzieri's perspective. What Tronti was proposing was not an opposition to capitalist development with the vague idea of mobilizing the workers democratically, but the workers' political power "against from within" capitalist development itself. As Panzieri had already emphasized, capitalist progress was tied to its need to extract a surplus from labor by reducing the possibilities of insubordination. Tronti argued for the necessity of going beyond this analysis, not by negating its premises, but by assuming them radically, from the workers' point of view. This point of view was the perspective of a class that recognized its power in its own capacity to forward capitalism's evolution by means of incessant struggle with it. The more advanced capitalism became, the more advanced the working class's capacity to attack would become. Lenin had translated Marx out of the context of the industrially advanced England of the nineteenth century into the backward Russia of the early twentieth century, believing from a tactical standpoint that the communist revolution would be most effective on the level of his country's underdevelopment. In the 1960s Tronti argued for bringing Lenin's revision of Marx back into a highly industrialized Europe. This idea, which he metaphorically referred to as "England" (where Marx wrote Das Kapital), was based on his belief that the proletariat was sufficiently mature and advanced at this point to direct a new communist revolution against the most advanced form of capitalism. This was one of the main hypotheses of the project of autonomy as elaborated by the Operaists. It took form in Tronti's first editorial-manifesto in <u>Classe operaia</u>, titled "Lenin in Inghilterra" (Lenin in England).[37] In a stylistically idiosyncratic manner, which from then on was to typify the one-sided stance not only of Operaism but of Autonomia as well (up through such recent manifestos as Hardt and Negri's <u>Empire</u>), Tronti affirmed:

> We too have worked with a concept that puts capitalist development first and workers second. This is a mistake. So now we have to turn the problem on its head, reverse the poles, and start again from the beginning: and the beginning is the class struggle of the working class. At the level of socially developed capital, capitalist development becomes subordinated to working-class struggles; it follows behind them, and they set the pace to which the political mechanisms of capital's own reproduction must be tuned.[38]

In order to understand better the theoretical premises of "Lenin in Inghilterra," though, we need to go back to Tronti's seminal essay "La fabbrica e la società" (Factory and society), published in the second issue of <u>Quaderni rossi</u>.[39] Referring to Marx, Tronti emphasized the two faces of capitalist production: the production process and the value process. In the first process, the workers use the machines; in the second, the machines use the workers. For this reason capitalism sees the production process as nothing more than capital, the transformation of labor into value. For Tronti, the main principle of capitalism's power is thus its ability to conflate "living labor" (workers' cooperation, the productive force that creates value) with "dead labor" (value in itself). This being the case, wrote Tronti,

> [C]apitalism identifies in its own way the unity between the process of producing goods and the process of producing value: the more it creates this unity, the more it develops, and the more it develops, the more the forms of capitalist production invade every sphere of society and proliferate within the whole network of social relations.[40]

But if from the capitalist's point of view the process of production and the process of creating value were strictly parallel and complementary, from the working-class perspective these two processes were clearly and sharply distinct in their unity. The workers' autonomy was thus the possibility of distinguishing between the process of work—themselves—and the process of value creation—capital—"to the point of putting one process against the other as two processes that ultimately contradict one another."[41] This meant opposing to capitalism's positive process of creating its own value the workers' negative process of creating value, which consisted of their will to be non-work, to refuse work, that is, to be the "material lever of capitalist dissolution placed at the decisive point of the system."[42]

Capitalism, according to Tronti, transformed the value of the labor force through a price that corresponded not to labor in its potential state, but to labor already accomplished; wage labor corresponded to labor completed. What capitalism was paying for, in other words, was performance, which was what maintained it as value within the system of capital. Capitalism's fundamental mystification is that it conceals the fact that the more the system of production moves toward newer forms of production, the more it blurs the distinction between the portion of work that has already been paid for and the portion that has not. According to Tronti, this mystification became the very concept of wage labor. Here existed the most powerful and totalizing mode of domination over the working class, namely the transformation of this class *de facto* by means of a concept that had been imposed on it, turning it from the basis of capital into a mere variable within the system. For this reason, Tronti proposed, as Panzieri had, to look beyond distribution and consumption as moments of exploitation, and to return—as Marx had insisted—to production as the fundamental moment in the relationship between the working class and capital, understood not simply as a process occurring within the factory, but extending outward from the factory to the entirety of social life.

For Panzieri, as we already have seen, production could not be reduced *sic et simpliciter* to the production of material goods. Production consisted of the organization of the social relations necessary to make labor power productive. Starting from this idea, Tronti argued that capitalist production tended constantly to go beyond itself in determining distribution, exchange, consumption, and all the relations among these moments. In spite of all the bourgeois mystifications, production was thus the structure of society. Society was a factory. As Tronti wrote:

> [T]he more capitalist development advances, which means the more the production of relative surplus extends itself, the more the capitalist cycle of production-distribution-consumption becomes one. At this point the relationship between bourgeois production and capitalist production, between society and the factory, and between society and the state, is organic. At the highest point of capitalist development, social production becomes a moment of the process of production, which means that all of society lives within the factory, and the factory extends its dominion over the whole of society.[43]

It was within this scenario of infinite extension of the concept of the factory—a concept that, as we shall see, was the premise for Archizoom's No-Stop City—that the factory disappeared as an actual place: "When the whole of society is reduced *de facto* to a factory, the factory as such tends to disappear. It is on this material basis, at a very high level, that the whole metamorphic process of bourgeois ideology comes to a conclusion."[44] The landscape in which this process was first enacted and conceptualized was the early twentieth-century capitalist metropolis. But if in the early stages the metropolis was a compact and concentrated artifact in opposition to the countryside, in its later stages it was more a territory. While many latter-day Marxists would read the features of this new metropolitan-territorial landscape as an Eden of consumption, Tronti and the Operaists saw it as integral to, and a projection of, the social means of production. This interpretation was possible only within the context of a rigorous reappropriation of Marx's insistence on production as the fundamental principle of society. It was from this principle—the principle of production—that Tronti established his project of autonomy.

In this context, the subjectivity of the workers became objectified as a force of capitalism, while industrial development was personified in the figure of the capitalist. From the capitalist perspective of the labor force as a mere commodity, the aim was to economize on the means of production, to produce more commodities with fewer commodities, a strategy that, as Panzieri

35

had already noted, meant that capitalist development constantly strove to reduce the number of workers while prolonging their working hours. For Tronti, it was on this ground that workers should found their own form of struggle. If the capitalists wanted to obtain more with less, the workers should aim to give them less for more—more money, that is, for less work. From this derived the possibility, for Tronti, of reversing the process of capitalist development in the direction of the workers' political autonomy:

> The working-class struggle has forced the capitalist to modify the form of his domination. This means that the pressure of the working class is able to force capitalism to change its internal composition. At this point the working class intervenes within the capitalist system as the essential component of its development.[45]

Here appeared clearly for the first time what was to constitute the focus of Tronti's theoretical work in the years to come: the autonomy of the political. Autonomy for Tronti implied not only a culture of conflict, but a technique of negotiation. Political negotiation was what established the rules that regulated the institutionalized struggle between capital and labor. It thus took place on ground that was not neutral but constituted by the relationship of forces between two adversaries. Nor could the power of the workers be based simply on an inherent capacity to resist capitalism. They also had to demand control of the institutions of negotiation, and in order to do so, they had to occupy the same political ground as the bourgeoisie—that of political institutions such as the Communist Party—because, as Tronti stated, "It is written nowhere that the political ground of the bourgeoisie will remain forever under the sky of capitalist society."[46] But in order to seize this possibility to engage in direct negotiation with capitalist institutions, the workers had to discover their own nature in the most radical way, through the very *form* of the working class, a discovery framed as a political project of crisis within capitalism's evolution.

Finally, in his book <u>Operai e capitale</u> (Workers and capital, 1966), Tronti clearly counterposed the two protagonists, the workers and the capitalists, as poles of an irreducible enmity. In this clash, what became the decisive political factor for the autonomy of the working class was the issue of work. As Marx had affirmed (and Tronti quotes), "[T]he subjective essence of private property, as subject, as person, is *work*."[47] The concept of private property invented by the capitalists was simply a reflection of the workers' expropriated labor. It was for this reason that, as Tronti noted, "since Adam Smith political economy has chosen labor as its principle. Labor is thus political economy's absolute measure—that is, its own abstraction."[48] Against this principle, Marx had recast the Hegelian notion of the labor force in political terms, taking labor not as an abstract category but as a subjective force expropriated from the worker. What economists identified as the costs of production were not the costs of production for work in itself, but rather the costs to keep workers in their state of potential labor. The difference between work and labor force boiled down to the fact that as producers of work the workers had no subjectivity of their own, while as members of the labor force they did. Accordingly, for Tronti it was no longer possible to talk about work but only about labor force. It was this latter concept that incarnated the autonomous subjective power of the worker against work, and thus against capital. "Labor as labor force already existed in Hegel," writes Tronti; "labor force as commodity already existed in Ricardo. The commodity labor force as a class of workers: this is Marx's discovery."[49]

Marx as the theoretical foundation, labor force as the reality of the workers, the working class as the political subject: it was this sequence of ideas that constituted Tronti's discovery of the workers' autonomous dimension. For Tronti, to rediscover Marx did not mean to prolong the tradition of Marxism, but to reconstruct Marx's original antagonism toward capitalism: the necessity of the working class as a precondition of the capitalist process of value creation and thus its ultimate threat. Within this conception, the political meaning of the working class became, simply, the negation of work.

This conception of the working class, of its presence, organization, and evolution, in itself constituted a strategy for refusing work and thereby for refusing capitalism. For Tronti, the strategy of refusal became the essence of the working class's identity. The strength of the working class was embodied not in the constructive positivity of work but rather in its refusal to *be* work; in other words, in an obstinate, destructive negativity, in a *de facto* demonstration of its intransigence toward its own transformation into wage labor. The refusal of work thus became the litmus test of the effectivity of the working class as a political body, an effectivity potentially much greater than that of its role in the evolution of capitalist production. Indeed, according to Tronti, the evolution of capitalism would henceforth be required to find its point of departure in the workers' negativity, in their identity as a fatal source of contradiction for capitalism rather than in their voluntary servitude as tokens of capitalist progress. This veritable Copernican revolution was envisioned by Tronti as completely overturning the concept of the political subject in relation to capitalist exploitation. If the force of the working class up until this point had been measured according to categories of resistance and reform of the status quo, Tronti saw in the workers' refusal, in their passive non-collaboration in the project of becoming capital—of becoming nothing but a labor force—the latent nucleus of true political emancipation and of radical autonomy from capitalist development.

It was only necessary, then, Tronti believed, to liberate the workers from capitalist reason and the capitalist myth of work. This process of liberation, which no longer viewed the working class as a class for labor but as a class for itself, could be attained only through a dissolution of preexisting thought. "Man, Reason, History," affirmed Tronti, "these monstrous divinities must be fought and destroyed."[50] But the work of dissolution was not to be the spontaneous *pars destruens* of someone who fights blindly against an enemy. It had to take on the sophisticated *Doppelcharakter* of a new kind of class struggle: "Theoretical reconstruction and practical destruction, from this moment on, cannot but run together like the legs of one and the same body."[51] Thus working-class nihilism toward forms of corporate society did not mean destruction for its own sake, but instead a real theoretical and strategic project of attaining emancipation and power through refusal and autonomy rather than adaptation and reform. As Tronti writes at the conclusion to <u>Operai e capitale</u>:

Tactics of organization in order to arrive at the strategy of refusal. It is between organization and refusal that the workers must insert their weapon in order to reduce capitalism to a subordinate force. This weapon consists of the workers' threat to negate their own essential mediation in the whole system of capitalist social relations. According to this, the tasks of the workers' party are: not to support capitalism's needs, not even in the form of workers' demands; to force the capitalists to present their objective necessities and then subjectively refuse them; to force the bosses to ask so that the workers can actively—that is, in organized forms—reply to them: no.[52]

Tronti and Cacciari: Autonomy of the Political and Negative Thought

At the end of the 1960s and in the 1970s the Autonomia groups applied this strategy literally. Under the influence of Antonio Negri, refusal changed from a tactic to be used by autonomous workers' organizations into an often anarchic, individualistic subversion undertaken for its own sake. Mario Tronti's scheme of putting the workers' struggle first and capitalist development second was applied mechanically to any transformation of capitalist organization, to the point of looking to the political crisis of the working-class movement in the 1970s as the ultimate challenge to advanced capitalism. Within the context of the capitalist restructuring of the assembly line, the mass worker became, according to Negri, the "social worker." If the working class was a politically strong subject, the "social worker" was the symptom of the proletarianization of an apolitical middle class. Against this scenario of increasing depoliticization, Tronti shifted his attention from the political possibilities existing within the advanced forms of capitalism toward the political *tout court,* understood as a counterstrategy to political economy. Already in Operai e capitale, however, Tronti had seen the strategy of the workers' refusal as the most extreme form—the ultimate instance of political autonomy, a strategy to be put in service of mobilizing the workers as an effective force with respect to capitalist production.

Therefore, the strategy of refusal should not be understood as an anarchic escape from work, but as only one of the tactics—the most radical one—within the overall political strategy of the workers' party. Following the experience of Classe operaia, which ceased publishing at the end of 1966, and the publication the same year of Operai e capitale, Tronti's focus turned to what had happened to the working class after Marx. Starting from the premise that Marxist theory was a radical critique of capitalist political economy but was not a theory of the political as such, Tronti analyzed the evolution of the working class from the opposite point of view. He focused on elaborating a history of the working class *per via negativa,* that is, a history written in terms of the political initiatives of capitalism, and consequently the State, to contain the pressure of the workers. It was precisely at moments when there was a "state of exception"—during a crisis, or when the workers' demands reached their highest level of intensity—that capitalism was forced to take the initiative politically and act with a certain independence from the economic determinants of its policies. In these rare but decisive moments, it was possible to see politics at work in a pure, autonomous form: as a friend/enemy struggle between capitalism and its adversary.

As Tronti stated in a seminar organized by Norberto Bobbio in 1972 at the faculty of political science in Turin, "The autonomy of the political is an expression which is common in political studies, but which sounds a bit strange and new in the ambit of a Marxist approach."[53] The immediate problem was to analyze not the degree of autonomy of one level from the other, but the autonomy of political power *tout court* with respect to economic determinations. Marxist tradition had always rejected any theory of political autonomy inasmuch as it denied the economic ground. It was for this reason that, according to Tronti, the "concept of the political" had to be introduced into Marxism as a "new category" that included both the objective ground of institutions established by the capitalist bourgeoisie and, at the same time, their subjective use, that is, their political actions. Behind this project lay Tronti's fundamental encounter with the thought of Carl Schmitt. As he would write much later, Schmitt was essential in order to politicize Marx radically, beyond both the analysis of political economy and of the political consequences of political economy—namely the critique of ideology—in order to arrive at an autonomous critique of power. Thus "Karl und

Carl," as he would title one of the chapters of his book La politica al tramonto (The sunset of politics): just as it was impossible to read Schmitt without Marx's discovery of the working class and its demystifying consequences, it was equally impossible to read Marx without Schmitt's definition of the political as a form of struggle.[54]

However, for Tronti it was also true—contrary to Schmitt's harsh criticism of all bourgeois forms of power—that it was only by a radical instrumentalization of the bourgeois cultural and political ground that a contemporary and more advanced project of antagonism to capitalism could be established. It was necessary to draw on what the great bourgeois thinkers had discovered in the relations between the bourgeoisie and capitalism, namely the role of *crisis* within the economic system and the ability of capitalism to internalize the collapse of the rigid teleological foundations of modern politics by means of a culture that systematically turned negativity into an engine of its own reproduction. For Tronti the latter did not amount simply to an economic mechanism of cause and effect, but a political dynamic conceived within the extremely advanced and sophisticated cultural outlook on modernity established by the bourgeoisie. Let the workers read Musil's great bourgeois novel instead of Mao's little red book, Tronti was suggesting. In other words, let the workers appropriate the very weapon that had so far been employed by the bourgeoisie as a means of achieving their defeat: the notion of negativity as an extreme form of capitalist mastery.

Adopting this point view miles away from the vulgarizations of Marxism and socialist struggle that were very much in fashion at the time, Tronti revisited the relationship between capitalism and politics in terms of a confrontation between a form of continuity and a form of discontinuity. What was continuous was the growth of the economy under capitalist domination; what was discontinuous was the workers' struggle and the capitalist counterstruggle. As Tronti claimed, "Economic continuity and political discontinuity *together:* this is the history of Capital."[55]

This position ultimately led Tronti to take a critical position toward Marx himself. For Tronti, Marx had failed to arrive at a full understanding of the relationship between the economic choices and the political choices that capitalism was forced to make in order to preserve its own continuity against the pressure of the workers. Against the classical economistic Marxist reading, Tronti affirmed the autonomy of political decision-making as an advanced way to practice the critique of ideology. By proceeding along this "scandalous" path, Tronti recognized that capitalism also evolved politically, through revolutions as well as other concrete projects of political autonomy. Faced with continual crises and the constant threat posed by the workers, capitalism had acquired over the course of its history a political specificity that contradicted its economic continuity.

Two historical events that were key examples for Tronti of this political specificity were Roosevelt's New Deal, on the one hand, and Keynes's economic theories, on the other, the latter of which apparently had an important influence on the American president's political handling of the biggest crisis capitalism had yet encountered. In the context of the New Deal, bourgeois culture discovered that the solution to the Great Depression lay not in the market but in politics. The second edition of Tronti's Operai e capitale, published in 1971, thus concluded not with a discussion of the workers' strategy of refusal but with its counterpart: the political development of capitalism under Roosevelt during the 1930s, understood as the most advanced answer to the then most advanced form of workers' struggle—the American working-class movement. According to Tronti, workers' struggles in the United States, unlike those in Europe, were focused not on revolution but on two pragmatic but politically consequential issues: increased wages and decreased working hours. As Tronti wrote: "It is for this reason that working-class struggles in America are much more serious than ours. They achieve many more things with less ideology."[56] Different from English capitalism, which was more advanced in its economic theory, and from German capitalism, which was more advanced in its cultural reflections, American capitalism was, for Tronti, much sharper and more advanced in its rare but crucial moments of institutional resolution of workers' struggles.

These were the moments that revealed the political core of the conflict between the workers and capital. For Tronti, the next step in the development of a workers' politics was to see the most durable and concrete forms of conflict as extending beyond ideological fixations on revolution and also beyond capitalism's counterrevolutionary response to the workers. It was for this reason that Tronti regarded American capitalism in the aftermath of the 1929 Depression as analogous not to the realized communism of the Soviet Union, but to the extremely realistic Social Democracy of Germany as that form of government took shape during the period of struggle from 1860 to 1913. In the conflict between German Social Democracy and the capitalist state there was, according to Tronti, such a radical avoidance of ideology that the system was able to undergo an extraordinarily lucid development, even if one that was politically not so appealing. Even without a political theory, and perhaps because of this, Social Democracy was able, in a highly realistic way, to take the content of the workers' struggle and translate it immediately into politics at the level of State institutions. As such, it constituted its party politics in a manner that went beyond Marx's critique of ideology, self-consciously adopting a tactical posture of compromise with its rival. For Tronti, this attitude paradoxically represented the highest and most effective form of autonomous political decision-making, leaving its mark not only on the workers' movement but also on the State, where the conflict between the workers and capitalists was institutionalized.

With a controversial *coup de théâtre,* then, the hyper-Leninist Tronti affirmed German Social Democracy as the paradigm of autonomous politics. If Lenin had proverbially disdained the petit-bourgeois realism of Social Democratic politics, Tronti felt no sense of contradiction in embracing it because, as he immediately emphasized, Lenin's Bolshevik revolution was nothing but a sequel to the advanced political thinking represented by the extreme realism of Germany's Social Democratic Party. It was within the experience of this party that bourgeois politics were reinvented as working-class politics. By going back to the politics of the working class in Germany and revealing that class's political autonomy, Tronti sought to demonstrate the transformative role of the working class within the history of modernity.

Thus, if the theoretical contribution of Quaderni rossi had

been focused on the concept of autonomy as a critique of technological development, and if Classe operaia had taken autonomy to be a form of workers' initiative, Tronti's subsequent reflections on the autonomy of the political turned the Operaist approach to the level of State institutions, posing a Marxist-Communist "counterplan" to the one of liberal capitalism. Around this hypothesis was launched the final journal of the Operaist movement, Contropiano. This represented the conclusion of Operaism's path toward working-class autonomy as a project dedicated to forging an alternative form of power to capitalism. Founded in 1968 by Asor Rosa, Cacciari, and Negri, Contropiano directed its theoretical and historical reflections to the relations among capitalist development, working-class history and practice, political institutions, and culture.

However, because of Contropiano's focus on the relationship between the working-class movement and political institutions such as the party, Negri registered his dissent from the group, leaving the journal after the first issue. Negri disagreed with Tronti's idea of the autonomy of the political as Tronti synthesized this position in his very first contribution to the journal, concerning the instrumentalization of the Communist Party for purposes of workers' politics.[57] Although Negri's concept of autonomy initially came directly out of Tronti's, their positions had increasingly diverged ever since the experience of Classe operaia. Their difference centered specifically on the political form of the workers' autonomy.

In order to understand this difference better, let us go back for a moment to the two most significant editorials of Classe operaia published in 1964, Tronti's "Lenin in Inghilterra" and Negri's "Operai senza alleati" (Workers without allies).[58] Tronti articulated the problem of the workers' political autonomy in terms of two distinct but at the same time interconnected levels of political action: tactics and strategies. If at the strategic level an autonomous revolution by the workers remained the goal, at the tactical one, as we have seen, Tronti's aim was the instrumentalization of party politics, understood by him as eventually offering the workers an opportunity to take power; like any other institution, he believed, the party was capable of being reappropriated by the workers as an "old tactic for a new strategy."[59] For Negri, on the other hand, the workers had no allies other than themselves. Thus, Negri's concept of the workers' refusal was incompatible with any process of political integration, first and foremost integration within the Communist Party. Tronti, however, never conceived his political extremism outside the framework of the party. It was political action *within* the institution, and eventually *against* it as the party made compromises against its own class interests, that constituted the very core of the Operaist philosophy.

More recently Tronti has admitted that he thought of the group around Classe operaia and Contropiano as a radical political elite acting outside the Communist Party but eventually taking it over and pushing it in the direction of a more radical political position.[60] It was in line with this ultimate strategy that the Contropiano project was supposed to develop. In other words, what was at stake in Contropiano was the development of a radical political class culture which, instead of taking for granted the imminent revolution—the first issue of the journal appeared just before the events of May 1968—opted for a longer-term, realistic counterplan to capitalism. For the contributors to Contropiano, a counterplan could not simply be conceived as a political intervention, but also, and especially, as a cultural and theoretical reflection. It was in this context that the journal forwarded its editorial line through broad theoretical considerations on such different fields as philosophy, architecture, and urbanism, and through vast genealogical projects of reconstruction aimed at an alternative history of bourgeois thought. This work was seen as a possible cultural weapon of the workers' movement. Among these projects, the most important and significant, especially if seen as philosophical and theoretical background to Tronti's autonomy of the political, was undoubtedly Massimo Cacciari's "Sulla genesi del pensiero negativo" (On the genesis of negative thought).[61]

This essay had its premises in Cacciari's reflections on the Weimar Republic's leftist organizations. The Venetian philosopher argued that the main cause of the workers' political defeat in Weimar Germany between 1917 and 1921 was the theoretical and practical inability of workers' organizations like the Communist Party and the Social Democractic Party to understand capitalism's politically productive use of crisis. Following Tronti, Cacciari considered that it was the instrumentalization of crisis, not the institution of rules, that enabled the bourgeoisie to control the political forces of capitalism. This political control took its theoretical form in what Cacciari called "negative thought." Understood by Cacciari as a form of postcapitalism, negative thought ultimately derived from the philosophies of Schopenhauer, Kierkegaard, and Nietzsche. It originated in a double refusal: on the one hand, a refusal of Romanticism, understood as a projection of the individual self into the world; on the other, a refusal of dialectics, understood as a grand synthesis of opposites that resolved the contradictions existing on the immanent plane of history. If Romanticism was an illusory celebration of contradictions staged as individual autonomy, dialectics was a manifestation of the act of negation recuperated as a positive by means of a process of contradiction and affirmation. It was because of its capacity to absorb contradictions as the mechanism of its continuous revolution that dialectics eventually won over an extreme form of refusal like Romanticism. For Cacciari, this capacity made Hegelian dialectics the ideal political form of the bourgeois state.

Hegel's State was the form that had to resolve within itself all social and political contradictions. Cacciari wrote:

> Art, Religion, the determinations of the subjective and objective spirit, the phenomenology of spiritual life—all these issues are incarnated by the dialectical process within its system. But what counts more is that History itself in all its modes (Tradition, Continuity, Progress) is now made the subject of an immanent conceptual analysis by the dialectical process. In this way, History loses any formal character, any teleological-subjective pretensions, in order to become the very substance of the functional unity between theory and praxis and a new form of human relationship.[62]

Dialectics was thus the basis of the political establishment of the bourgeois state, which saw itself as the only supreme historical synthesis, the only conceivable universal set of values. But with the development of capitalism and the increasing threat of the proletariat that emerged within it, dialectics became the defensive position of an entity that was unable to go beyond its opposite and therefore opted for a dialogue with it. Therefore, according to Cacciari, the tradition of negative thought was an attempt to challenge dialectics from within, to challenge the very form responsible for the enduring power of bourgeois capitalism. This tradition had transformed the negative—the internal opposition between bourgeois values and capitalism's tumultuous revolution, which destroyed in its wake any pretended or presumedly established values—into the very engine of a culture that was finally able to master capitalism by internalizing its deep causes.

According to Cacciari, the high point of this process of negation was represented by Nietzsche's radical concept of the will to power and Max Weber's notion of disenchantment. With Nietzsche, the Hegelian will to a dialectical synthesis of opposites was replaced by the unbalanced force of the will to power, a force that shaped existence itself. In its act of forming the world, the will to power did not involve a search for justification in any notion of universality; rather, it absolutely refused any set of values, aesthetic, ethical, or religious. As a supreme form of bourgeois ideology, negative thought prepared the ground for an acceptance of the state of permanent instability brought about by capitalism. With Weber, bourgeois disenchantment with capitalism's hegemonic power was conceived as the only possibility of bourgeois political power. Weber thus translated Nietzsche's will to power into an ultimate acceptance of the bourgeoisie's destiny as total integration within the iron cage of capitalist development.

For Cacciari, however, it was this disenchanted state of acceptance that constituted the bourgeoisie's ideological superiority. As such, in order to penetrate this construct of bourgeois power within capitalism, it was crucial to appropriate its mode of thinking. Cacciari writes: "Only by reading Nietzsche and Weber together do we finally discover how the tragic negativity can resolve itself positively and, at the present historical level reached by capitalism, as the only possible condition of the functionality of ideology."[63] This existential and cultural understanding of bourgeois ideology as the engine of capitalism was, in Cacciari's view, a correct understanding of the irreversibility of the capitalist process. Accordingly, its transformation was a necessary prerequisite to the political mastery of capitalist development.

For both Cacciari and Tronti, then, the only possibility of autonomy for the working class was the appropriation of the negative mode of bourgeois thinking, beyond all the ethical, ideological, and cultural resistance that leftist culture had toward this legacy. It was within this spirit that Tronti, in his first article published in Contropiano, "Estremisti e riformisti" (Extremists and reformists), declared that neither reformist nor extremist political attitudes could be the weapon of the working-class movement with respect to the negative *modus operandi* of capitalism since the latter had the capacity to absorb and finally resolve every crisis within its structures. Instead, the working-class movement had to embrace capitalism as a form of development, but on one crucial condition: that this class finally assume the will to power over itself. If capitalism meant development, then the working class—the class of producers—must become empowered. As Tronti writes:

> We have to courageously assume the principle that not only does capitalism need the working class, but the working class also needs capitalism. Not only do the workers need capitalism to achieve their own political maturity, but society in general also needs capitalism for the sake of its own development. If capital is the modern form of development, the working class is the modern form of power. These corollaries must become the new conditions of the workers' struggle.[64]

From this position, then, it became crucial to construct an antagonist culture that could also envision the possibility of its own institutionalization. The project of Contropiano was therefore not so much centered on a political-economic critique of politics but, on the contrary, on a political critique of political economy and its stubborn assumption of economics as the primary determinant of historical development. It was time to abandon the emphasis on the critique of ideology for a theory of power, one focused not only on politics but also on culture at the level of philosophy and especially of architecture and the city.

It was this perspective that framed the participation, starting in 1969, of a group of architectural historians gathered around Manfredo Tafuri at the IUAV (Istituto Universitario di Architettura di Venezia), where Tafuri in 1968 had founded the Istituto di Storia. Yet Tafuri's seminal essay "Per una critica dell'ideologia architettonica" (Toward a critique of architectural ideology),[65] which was meant to be the institute's methodological blueprint and was included in the same issue in which Cacciari published his essay on negative thinking, was still closely tied to exactly what Contropiano intended to go beyond: the critique of ideology. The critique of ideology was seen by Tronti, Cacciari, and Asor Rosa as only a precondition for political work, not a conclusion to it. For them, the conclusion was what the title of the magazine was already proposing: a counterplan, to be elaborated in the form not of a critique, but of a *theory*. What the practice of the critique of ideology had taught the Operaists was how to demystify the way capitalist development had previously been theorized by capitalists and sometimes by Marxists. Their great discovery consisted in the fact that what made capitalist development strong was not its continuity, but its discontinuity: its ability to absorb the negative, that which at first seemed to be its opposite or its collateral effects. Capitalist cultural politics, as Tafuri would say, assuaged bourgeois anxiety through an internalization of its causes.[66] However, once this mechanism was discovered, it was necessary for a culture antagonistic to capitalism to make use of this mechanism productively and deliberately, even when such use would seem to have a regressive horizon. *A theory of the use of the critical effects of capitalism* was the complement to the critique of ideology.

In this sense, it is possible to see a discrepancy between Tafuri's critique of architectural ideology and the project of political autonomy elaborated by Tronti and Cacciari. This discrepancy is exemplified by Tafuri's essay "Austromarxismo e città: 'Das rote Wien,'" (Austro-Marxism and the city: "red Vienna").[67] In this contribution to Contropiano, in which Tafuri sought to apply the critique of ideology he had outlined in his 1968 book Teorie e storia dell'architetture (Theories and history of architecture) (written prior to his arrival in Venice and his close involvement with the Contropiano circle), the architectural historian produced a careful history of Red Vienna, analyzing the attempt by the Social Democratic municipality of Vienna to plan and build new social housing between 1920 and 1930 and reading this episode in the context of the ideology of "Austro-Marxism." The latter was a movement of Austrian political thinkers who, from their socialist position, sought to recalibrate Marxism with democratic politics and capitalist reality as the inevitable path of social development. Tafuri's aim in his essay, however, was to go beyond the "image" of these social housing projects built during the period of Hitler's *Anschluss* as a working-class fortress against Nazism in order to disentangle the relationships existing among the thought of Austro-Marxist political thinkers (like Otto Bauer, Rudolf Hilferding, and Max Adler), the urban initiatives of the Vienna municipality, and the specific formal language adopted by the architects of the typical Red Vienna social housing blocks, including Peter Behrens and Karl Ehn.

Tafuri began his critique by observing that what was singular about Austro-Marxism was its distinction between Marxist theory, understood by the Austro-Marxists as a scientific theory of the laws of social development, and socialism, understood as an ethical principle, as ideology. He thus emphasized the Austro-Marxists' neo-Kantian approach to the political; for them, politics was an act of mediation between two irreducible poles: the realm of necessity—that is, the "natural" conditions of the economy—and the realm of duty—that is, the collective will to socialism. Socialism for the Austro-Marxists was "a moral ideal directly confronting the objectivity of the capitalist order."[68] In Tafuri's view, this distinction between the objectivity of the economic and the subjectivity of the political was responsible for the ultimate failure of the politicians of the Vienna municipality to produce real reform. While the Austro-Marxists succeeded in having their social housing program implemented in the nation's capital, the dualism between economics and politics prevented the Social Democratic Party from undertaking any deeper reform of the economic system it had inherited from the bourgeoisie. Instead of following the radical political path of Soviet Russia, or the more structural reforms attempted by the Social Democratic Party in Germany, Bauer and his fellows remained concerned with finding a balance between socialist goals and democratic consensus—indeed, with what in contemporary political terms might be called a "third way." This required of the Austro-Marxists a high degree of *Realpolitik* vis-à-vis the preexisting capitalist organization of the city. Thus, building the socialist city meant first building the symbols of the new city rather than radically rethinking its economic and organizational premises. Indeed, what was remarkable about Red Vienna was its attempt to change the form of the city without first reforming the economic program of the State.

This Viennese "detachment" of urban politics from economic planning was the exact opposite of that represented by Ludwig Hilberseimer's *Groszstadtarchitektur* at around the same time. Tafuri repeatedly asserted that Hilberseimer's theoretical proposal for a modern metropolis designed element by element, from the single cell to the entire urban organism, was the only modern urban project to reflect lucidly upon the new totalizing dimension implicit in the capitalist integration of the city. Compared to this model, all other attempts to design the city by means of delimited, architecturally determined forms appeared to Tafuri romantic and outdated, indeed "regressive utopias." Red Vienna represented not a cohesive, organic replanning of the city, in his view, but instead an archipelago of [31] urban artifacts— monumental *Höfe* (courtyards)—which, while "negotiating" their position in the leftover spaces of the city, sought to confront the existing city with exceptional monuments of thematic coherence. Thus Red Vienna was nothing more than an example of "ideology realized" for Tafuri, the outcome of an urban *mise-en-scène* rather than a real plan for change. It was in light of his exasperation with ideology that Tafuri read such projects as the building blocks of Behrens for the Winarskyhof [32] (1924–26) and Ehn for the Karl-Marx-Hof (1927–30), among others. Although he incisively praised the formal qualities of these buildings, even emphasizing their avoidance of gratuitous populist expressionism, Tafuri nonetheless found their epic architecture insufficient to construct a real alternative to the existing city. Not even their proposal of superblocks located in proximity to the city center—challenging the tendency to "suburbanization" represented by contemporary low-density workers' settlements such as the housing projects of Adolf Loos—appeared to Tafuri a valid alternative to the capitalist reorganization of urban geography.

In Tronti's view, however, Tafuri's critique of ideology in the context of his analysis of Red Vienna was too mechanical, too anchored in the concept of economic planning as the sole mode of capitalist advancement.[69] According to Tronti, what appeared to Tafuri as a regressive utopia in Vienna was instead a rare ability on the part of the Social Democratic municipality to exploit the dire economic and political conditions of Austria after World War I and thereby to begin to build a socialist city from within but against the forms of the bourgeois city. We should not forget that although the Social Democrats controlled the municipal administration, they constituted the minority opposition party in the National Parliament. This situation made Vienna a "state of exception" in which the municipality was literally advancing urban policies in opposition to the national ones, with all the strategic political symbolism that this situation implied.

The postulation of an archipelago of monumental artifacts as an alternative to the master planning of the entire city was thus not simply a matter of clever compromises in order to achieve the best possible outcome—which for Tronti would still constitute a manifestation of the autonomy of the political—but a very advanced urban design proposal. As a rejection of the total planning of the capitalist city, it incorporated this approach by means of its very negativity, that is, its irreducibility to a dialectical process, its production of a site of permanent crisis and confrontation. In line with the theoretical premises of negative thought, the monuments of Red Vienna represented, in sum, an expression of the will to form. Clearly contrasting with the existing city while at the same time presuming to be the expression of the dominant class, these monumental impositions were for Tronti a coherent and "realistic" way of dealing with the "objective" conditions of capitalism. Tafuri, on the other hand, refused to credit this crucial aspect of Austro-Marxism as applied to the urban design of socialist Vienna. He took a negative view of the municipality's willingness to compromise, its apparently backward urban politics, its call for a new workers' monumentality, and its will to action and power within the fragmented context of the metropolis, without recourse to the abstraction of a general plan, of a total programming of the *Groszstadt*.

Yet Red Vienna was a clear manifestation of what the Operaists were searching for beyond the critique of ideology: namely, the autonomy of political action and its primacy with respect to the capitalist evolution of society. For the Operaists, the autonomy of the political meant a careful tuning of Marxist politics to the irreducible singularity of the places where those politics were applied. Not an overall plan for the city but rather a theory of the city was, in their view, the only concrete means to advance an alternative to capitalist planning. If bourgeois power in the city was shaped by exceptions and singularities rather than systems and programs, these same exceptions and singularities could potentially become forms representing the autonomous power of the workers. But such an approach required an entirely different reading of the city. It required an understanding of the city as a place of political formation—of contingencies, actions, and exceptions—rather than as a place based on abstract mechanisms of planning and development. It is within this perspective that Aldo Rossi's conception of an autonomous architecture firmly based on the idea of the singularity of the *locus* rather than on the science of planning came close to the Operaists' conclusions—paradoxically enough, much closer than did Tafuri's critique of ideology.

Rossi: The Concept of the *Locus* as a Political Category of the City

The construction of an alternative to the capitalist city and the proposal of an autonomous architectural culture thus meant, above all, the constitution of a theory of the city. In the 1950s Italian architecture had been mainly a matter of increasing *professionalismo* (literally, professionalism). It was an attempt to link a still artisanal dimension of design and building techniques with the urgent demands of modernization created by the rapid advance of postwar capitalist development. In the 1960s, however, with the reemergence of political struggles and new social conflicts, the necessity appeared in all disciplines, including within the internal discourse of architecture and urbanism, to find a way toward cultural and conceptual renewal. Instead of simply advancing in tandem with the further modernization of architecture and the city, the need for renewal became visible as a demand for a theoretical refoundation of architecture in relation to the city.

In the 1950s and early 1960s the main protagonists of the intellectual debate in architecture had been Bruno Zevi, an architectural historian, critic, and founder of the Movement for Organic Architecture (APAO); Giulio Carlo Argan, an art historian and author of several important contributions to the theory and historiography of modern architecture; and Ernesto Nathan Rogers, an architect and leader of the BBPR office and director of the prestigious magazine Casabella continuità from 1953 to 1964. Their contributions may be summed up as a critical recuperation and cultural reinvention of the theoretical objectives of the Modern Movement, especially as the latter were represented by three different directions: Frank Lloyd Wright's organic architecture (supported by Zevi), Walter Gropius's pedagogical program at the Bauhaus (supported by Argan), and the ethical legacy of CIAM (supported by Rogers).[70] This recuperation was to some degree intended by all three theorists as a political project, aimed at a new cultural and historical legitimation of the liberal trajectory of the Modern Movement as the only path to a democratic architecture and city.

But it was against the ideological pretensions of this nexus of liberalism, democracy, and modernism that the refoundation of architectural theory would take form in the 1960s in the thinking of the next generation, above all architects like Aldo Rossi and Andrea Branzi, both born in the 1930s and reaching intellectual maturity at this moment. For these new protagonists, the cultural proposals advanced by intellectuals like Zevi, Argan, and Rogers were still bound to a reformist view of the relationship between politics and architectural thought. They aimed at a recovery of the modern city in terms of the negative political, cultural, and formal instrumentalities and ideologies that had been brought into being by capitalist development: respectively, spatial humanism as a way of making the new forms of habitation more acceptable, new technologies as a way of distributing social equality, and coexistence between the old and the new as a way of manifesting an ethical pluralism. What these committed intellectuals did not, and could not, put into question was their own unwavering trust in the continuing progress of democracy; they were unable to question the structural foundations of this assumption. The basis of the postwar democratic city—both the real one and the one imagined by these "liberal" architectural thinkers—was not simply the political economy of capitalism, however, but also its ideological representations. The latter especially took the form of a rediscovered "humanism," which became the mantra of socially *engagé* intellectuals.

With the rhetorical abuse and exhaustion of professionalism and humanism in the early 1960s, and in the face of the advancing process of integration of social relations within the context of contemporary capitalist development, there were, in the view of the new generation of intellectuals, two theoretical paths that appeared as potentially valid alternatives in architecture: on the one hand, a political affirmation of the autonomy of architectural *poiesis* in the form of the reinvention of categories such as typology and place (Rossi); and on the other, a critique of the ideology of the capitalist city as this ideology manifested itself in the postwar recuperation of the Modern Movement and a new wave of technological avant-gardism in the 1960s (Tafuri and Branzi). In spite of their sometimes radical differences, these two positions may be said to have converged in the necessity of a theory that consisted not in the autonomy of the discipline, but in the autonomy of a political subject committed to the formulation of a cultural alternative to the bourgeois domination of the capitalist city. Theory was always against ideology, as Tronti affirmed in these years. If ideology coincided with the blind belief in progress, with faith in the evolution of society for the better, theory, as Tronti quoted from Paul Klee, was *sichtbar machen*—making visible, that is, the construction of a clear analytical and political point of view based on the solid ground of concrete conceptual categories.[71] But in making visible what was invisible, theory was also meant to go beyond the critique of ideology, to resolve itself in the project. It was in this sense that in 1966 Rossi, just after completing his book L'architettura della città, declared at a symposium organized by the school of architecture in Venice:

The creation of a theory is the first objective of an architectural school, prior to all other types of research. A design theory is the most important moment of every form of architecture; thus, in an architectural school, the course in theory should be the driving force in the curriculum. It is remarkable how rarely one encounters theories of architecture or, in other terms, rational explanations of how to make architecture. One stumbles across only a few writings on this matter, by either the most naive or else the most outstanding individuals. Above all, one notices how those who adopt a few principles of a theoretical type become so uncertain about them as to avoid trying to verify them, which is the most important moment of any theory—in other words, to establish a relationship between the theory and making of architecture. In the end, one can only say this: that for some a theory is only a rationalization of a previous action; therefore, it tends to be a norm rather than a theory. At the risk of appearing naive, my proposal is to outline a true and appropriate theory of architecture, in other words, to form a theory of design as an integral part of a theory of architecture.[72]

Having been deeply influenced by the writings of Antonio Gramsci, especially Gramsci's reflections on the role of intellectuals—whom the political philosopher had defined as autonomous yet organically linked to party institutions and thus responsible for the creation of its hegemonic forms of culture—Rossi joined the Italian Communist Party in 1956, at the time of the Twentieth Party Congress in the Soviet Union and the invasion of Hungary, a moment when many leftist intellectuals were instead leaving the party. His intellectual formation between 1954 and 1964 as a politically engaged architecture student and regular contributor to Rogers's magazine Casabella continuità included the writing of a series of articles in which he came to see architecture no longer as a product of masters but as an integral part of the evolution of urban phenomena.[73] Carlo Aymonino, an architect who directed the design department of the IUAV in the 1970s and was close to Rossi, has said that what characterized their generation was primarily the replacement of architectural history interpreted within an art-historical perspective by urban history understood in relation to political development.[74] If this is so, then we may say that Rossi represented a paradigmatic case, and his pioneering essays on Milanese neoclassicism and the architecture of the Enlightenment, his monographic writings on architects like

Loos and Behrens, and his case studies of cities like Berlin, Hamburg, and Vienna aimed to establish a new, autonomous field of research in which architectural form was conceived as the primary means of constituting the politics of the modern city.

Rossi's hypothesis of autonomous architecture involved more than the rejection of the naiveté of functionalism, nor was it just a call for disciplinary specificity. It was rather a search for a rational language: a theory of form liberated from the sequence of formal styles in the service of the dominant bourgeois institutions. His rediscovery of the architecture of rationalism was an attempt to recuperate and reappropriate the legacy of the bourgeois city as the form of the socialist city. In his first important essay, entitled "Il concetto di tradizione nel neoclassicismo milanese" (The concept of tradition in the architecture of Milanese neoclassicism),[75] he analyzed the relationship between the politics of the Napoleonic government of Milan and its specific architectural language. This language had its formal expression in the Jacobin rationalism of Luigi Antolini's design for the Foro Bonaparte. What Rossi saw in this architecture, and in other monumental buildings and urban interventions of Napoleonic Milan, was the will of the bourgeoisie to assert and represent itself as the dominant new class vis-à-vis the old aristocracy. The architecture of the neoclassical city was thus for Rossi primarily a political choice by the Milanese bourgeoisie concerning the new institutions of power, who understood them as means to define and realize its idea of public space. The bourgeois class thus gave expression to its existence and status through its appropriation and reinvention of the classical tradition. In Rossi's view, it was time for the socialist city to likewise construct its own tradition by appropriating and reinventing the legacy of *its* predecessor, namely the city of the bourgeoisie.

It was in the context of his effort to define the civic realism of a socialist architecture that Rossi revisited the history of European bourgeois rationalism from the eighteenth to the twentieth century—from Boullée to Loos. This project reached its theoretical culmination in 1973 with Rossi's organization and curatorship of the Fifteenth Triennale in Milan, which Rossi devoted to a survey on "rationalist" architecture in the twentieth 24, 25 century, both before and after World War II.[76] In contrast to the general design exuberance of the 1960s, Rossi reappropriated the tradition of rationalism not in the fashion of the Modern Movement, as a normative and functional language, but rather as an affirmation of a potentially autonomous architecture opposed to the hybrid and technologically heteronomous forms being churned out by neocapitalist urbanism at this time. In commenting on his choice of references and examples for the Triennale, Rossi wrote: "[W]e have here incorporated some texts by and references to Ludwig Hilberseimer, Adolf Behne, and Hans Schmidt because they have a particular meaning within the legacy of the Modern Movement. These texts are valid because they have confronted the contradictions of bourgeois architecture from a socialist perspective."[77]

For Rossi it was important to continue the modern tradition of Hilberseimer, Behne, and Schmidt not as a generic and open-ended movement, but as a political and cultural project, a *tendenza*[78]—a recognizable architectural development aiming to establish an alternative to the capitalist city. Within this framework, what was needed, according to Rossi, was not a change of architectural style or urban form, but the elaboration of a new theoretical point of view on the city and architecture. Its aim should be the primacy of political choices over technocratic ones. In this sense, Rossi's elaboration of an autonomous architecture coincided with his proposal of a theory of the city capable of challenging what he saw in the early 1960s as capitalism's new form of urban project: its totalistic planning of the city, with its concomitant celebration of technology. For Rossi, the premise of a contemporary theory of the city should be the city as a site of political choices—as a concrete geography of places irreducible to the totality and continuity of urbanization.

A fundamental testing ground for Rossi's theoretical challenge to late-capitalist urbanity was his first teaching experience as a tutor in the advanced course of urbanism organized by the Olivetti Foundation in Arezzo in 1963. Conceived as a specialized program for postgraduate students, the Arezzo advanced course was conducted by important figures within the Italian urban debate such as Ludovico Quaroni and Giancarlo de Carlo. Among the younger tutors, besides Rossi himself, it included the participation of Paolo Ceccarelli—an urbanist and the translator of Kevin Lynch's The Image of the City—and Tafuri, at that time a militant young historian and architect involved in a newly established collaborative of architects and planners called AUA (Architetti Urbanisti Associati), which was inspired by the professional *modus operandi* of American practices like Gropius's TAC and Skidmore, Owings & Merrill. The theme of the advanced course was the updating of the discipline in the face of the changes that had occurred within Italian cities and their surrounding territory under the pressure of the economic boom of the 1950s and early 1960s and the accompanying massive immigration from the poor south to the industrialized north. This disciplinary updating, underwritten by the Olivetti Foundation, was carried out in the context of a newly formed Center-Left national coalition strongly focused on economic programming, urban planning, and other new urban initiatives.[79]

Within this perspective in which urbanism was understood to be the horizon where all the design disciplines converged, the two goals of the Arezzo course were, first, an elaboration and discussion of new techniques inspired by the tradition of town planning and, second, the conceptualization of a "new urban dimension" beyond the traditional form and confines of the historical city. Just one year before, in 1962, Tafuri and Giorgio Piccinato, in an important essay published in Casabella continuità, had proposed the concept of the "city-territory" as an innovative framework within which to study the recent transformations of the urban landscape.[80] The main emphasis of their contribution, in both their essay and the course, was the paradigm of the territory as an open form created by the complex new network of transportation and other economic flows. According to Tafuri and Piccinato, the primary consequence of the new modes of industrial production was the increasing integration of the city and countryside into a single entity, creating a new territorial scale and role.

Tafuri's and Piccinato's position in the Arezzo course therefore emerged within the institutional Left's consciousness of the increasing importance of new planning devices, understood as rigorously "scientific" methods for integrating economic programming and territorial planning. Indeed, one of the political objectives of this Center-Left coalition, and especially of the Socialist Party, was the rationalization of the means of capitalist production and distribution in the interests of attaining a more balanced social system. This balanced capitalism received a precise and categorical formal definition: that of the "city-territory."[81] Viewed within the political framework of the increasing expansion of capitalism to the entire social spectrum, this category of the city-territory—presented by many leftist planners and architects (including Tafuri and Piccinato) as the ultimate destiny of urban evolution—was not politically neutral. Underlying it was an affirmation of the mutated modes of production created by the transition from a purely competitive to a more organized—oligarchic or monopolistic—form of capitalism. This new capitalism imposed the need for greater logistical coordination among cities, centers of industrial production, and the urban territory lying between them.

Rossi's polemical stance against the category of the city-territory in both the Arezzo course and L'architettura della città became the basis of his proposal for an alternative urban theory founded on the idea of the *locus.* Interpreted in the cultural and political context in which he was writing, the *locus* must be understood as a concept aimed directly at countering the processes of capitalist integration. But before further analyzing Rossi's position, let us see how the radical Left reacted to theoretical proposals such as the city-territory as presented in the Arezzo course. A very interesting reaction was that of Claudio Greppi and Alberto Pedrolli in an article entitled "Produzione e programmazione territoriale" (Production and territorial planning), published in the third issue of Quaderni rossi.[82] Militants of Operaism and students at the school of architecture in Florence, Greppi and Pedrolli emphasized how the new concept of the city-territory represented a qualitative leap in capitalism's strategic process of appropriation of the city. According to the authors, the capitalist instrumentalization of urban design had had the effect during the first half of the twentieth century of fragmenting and dispersing the labor force throughout the territory, favoring regressive forms like the Garden City and the rural neighborhood. After World War II, the typical examples of Italian social housing included the many complexes built under the auspices of INA-Casa, an institution established by the Christian Democrats to shelter "those who work."[83] The plans of INA-Casa and other housing organizations were likewise fragmentary and incremental, and they continued to be based on the notion of the self-sufficient, decentralized neighborhood unit. With the advent of neocapitalism, however, according to Greppi and Pedrolli, the need to better integrate the workers—who were being transformed from a simple industrial force into a social one—with the forces of production caused the strategies of fragmentation to be supplanted by those of territorial coordination. In this sense, as Greppi and Pedrolli wrote, "the obsolete concept of the self-sufficient satellite city still reacting to a static relationship between city and countryside is replaced by the city-territory, understood as a structure that organizes the totality of the urban territory in order to make it more productive."[84]

Greppi and Pedrolli accused the "young leftist theorists" of urbanism of taking for granted the category of the city-territory as a neutral and progressive representation of the human habitat. "Behind the definition of the city-territory," Greppi and Pedrolli stated, "there is only the attempt to integrate the labor force more within the development of capitalism, this time not through repression but through democratic institutions and even through the battles of the Left for greater social justice."[85] As such, the only alternative to the idea of the city-territory, in their view, was not its socialist reappropriation, but rather an autonomous appropriation of the city as it was. This autonomous appropriation was identified by the authors not as a new urban planning project but as the taking over of already established working-class typologies. The fortress-type buildings constructed by the Social Democratic municipality of Red Vienna as a counter to the unlimited extension of the city, discussed above, would be one example of this approach. Typologies were concrete urban signs, according to Greppi and Pedrolli, the representation of a concrete and precise political choice in opposition to presumed "scientific" planning. Against the social integration of the capitalist city, democratically absorbed by the developing forces of production, Greppi and Pedrolli proposed a city of parts identified with a geography of working-class resistance to such integration. Their proposal was very similar to both Operaism's political critique and to Rossi's architectural critique of the urban category of the city-territory. During the seminar Rossi strongly opposed the use of categories from the contemporary planning discourse that he saw as products of a blind and positivistic faith in urban development. Against the mystification of the city-territory—which was put forward in Arezzo by Tafuri and endorsed by Quaroni and de Carlo—Rossi insisted on the concreteness of the urban artifact, of the architecture of the city, as the most relevant and precise instrument of urban analysis and design. Instead of looking to the city as an undefined, neutral ground shaped only by the categories imposed by the accelerating forces of urbanization, Rossi proposed to see the city as a place formed by politics. From this standpoint, only an analysis of architecture could reveal the city's immanent separateness, that is, its constitution of parts not reducible to the common denominator of technological development.

The two conceptual categories of such an analysis were typology, understood as knowledge concerning the constitution and evolution of urban forms; and the individuality of the urban artifact, understood as the concreteness of architecture in its actual material manifestation. If typology for Rossi was the "science" through which it was possible to assess the nature and evolution of the city according to an analysis irreducible to any monolithic idea of urban development, the individuality of the urban artifact was the moment of decision in which typological principles were applied to the real city. The field in which typology met the individuality of the urban artifact was neither urban planning, with its abstract, diagrammatic representations, nor "townscape," with its iconic representations of urban scenes, but rather urban geography, with its concept of the *locus.* By *locus* Rossi meant the geographic singularity of architecture's constitution, understood not just as empirical evidence but as a universal structural condition.

Greppi has recently recalled that a major appeal of Rossi's position for the radical Left was his strong interest, unusual among architects at the time, in urban geography as a critical framework opposed to townscape.[86] During these years Rossi was intensely studying the major authors of the French urban geography school, including Marcel Poëte, Maurice Halbwachs, Jean Tricart, Georges Chabot, and Max Sorre. These scholars were interested in reading urban space both as a field of fragmenting forces and as a whole whose evolution still had a discernible structure. With his reference to the studies of Sorre, Rossi construed the idea of *locus* as a manifestation of singular points within the overall framework of the city. As he writes in a crucial passage of L'architettura della città, "[A] geographer like Sorre could suggest the possibility of a theory of spatial division and, based on this, postulate the existence of 'singular points.' The *locus,* so conceived, emphasizes the conditions and qualities within undifferentiated space which are necessary for understanding an urban artifact."[87] In this sense, it is possible to say that for Rossi the *locus* constituted the very limit of any intervention or interpretation of the city.

In his opposition to planning and his defense of the idea of the *locus,* Rossi thus implicitly opposed the techno-capitalist conception of urbanization latent in planning practice. The city was a plurality of parts that did not add up to any totality, especially one imposed by the capitalist forces of integration. In this sense, it was possible to interpret the category of place as a *political* category, which, by virtue of the separateness that it evoked, *de facto* opposed the broad-scale subjugation of the territory to the totalizing forces of capitalist development. The embrace of the *locus* and of other concepts similarly characterized by their singular nature—for example, monumentality and collective memory, so pervasive throughout L'architettura della città—thus should be understood not as an effort to recuperate a traditional view of the city, but instead to establish a new political reading. By proposing a lucid theory that rendered the city immune to the anxiety of capitalist change and innovation, Rossi seemed to be suggesting that there was a possibility of looking at the city as an arena of decisive and singular events whose defined forms could pose a challenge to the urban phenomena and flux surrounding them.

At the same time, it was possible to use this theory to analyze these singular events in terms of their deeper structural consequences, in terms of their profound role in the collective experience of the city. To look at the city as a manifestation of a collective urban memory was to go beyond what was empirically visible and perceive the dialectical conflict between constituent and constituted forces. In this sense, demolitions, reconstructions, and disruptions became events through which the actual history of the city could be traced. According to Rossi, these phenomena were what really constituted urban development. In this context, the aim of an autonomous theory of the city was to assess the real dynamic of discontinuous events, beyond their iconic visibility, beyond the superficial image of the city. Thus Rossi titled his book L'architettura della città. Both inspired by and critical of Kevin Lynch's book The Image of the City, published six years earlier,[88] Rossi proposed *architecture* instead of *image* as a way to go beyond a thin perceptual-psychological reading of the city. While taking empirical evidence—the individuality of the urban fact—as his point of departure, Rossi insisted that the architectural study of the city should emphasize both the geographic continuities that functioned as structuring elements within the city and the historical discontinuities that characterized the city's evolution. Within such a study, the *locus,* understood as a universal condition of singularity, functioned as the conceptual framework.

Rossi first articulated his conception of the *locus,* which, as we have just suggested, became one of the bases of his rejection of the category of the city-territory and of the uncritical affiliation of the urban structure with the forces of capitalist production, in a text cowritten with some colleagues at the school in Venice and presented in 1965 at the nineteenth congress of the Istituto Nazionale Urbanistica (INU).[89] It may be read as one of the Venice Group's most important early collective efforts. It was Rossi's insistence on the anti-technocratic categories of place, typology, and urban artifact that would later constitute the Scuola di Venezia's main methodological axis. Among the specific polemical targets of the group led by Rossi were such *au courant* concepts as the "open project" and the "network" as well as the preoccupation among urbanists and architects with informational technologies and cybernetics. Against the uncritical use of these concepts, the Venice group wrote,

It is difficult, if not impossible, to define the formal and spatial terms of urban transformation within the presumed global vision of planning because planning often presumes a demiurgic design of the entire territory.... From the point of view of the design of the city it is difficult to understand the exact meaning of expressions such as "open project." These expressions are similar to such very fashionable aesthetic categories as "open form," and they are mystifications in view of the fact that any design intervention addresses a problem by means of a form. It is only the possibility of a closed, defined form that permits other forms to emerge.[90]

Against the presumed open-ended form of city-territory planning, then, Rossi's group opposed an urban space of finite, juxtaposed parts. The limitation implied by the circumscribed form of the urban artifact was seen as the foundation of the architecture of the city. Within this theoretical position, the architectural project was understood as autonomous vis-à-vis the city, yet not detached from it; on the contrary, the singular intervention had a clearly articulated relationship to the overall social and political context. This mode of thinking was counterposed by Rossi and his colleagues to the so-called organic tradition of planning, represented by the work and theories of figures like Patrick Geddes, Gaston Bardet, Lewis Mumford, and Victor Gruen. Within this tradition, the urban territory was regarded as constituted by the organic growth of flexible organisms evolving in relation to the technological development of the infrastructure. The determinism implied in this model made it a natural representation of bourgeois class values and ideology. What Rossi and his colleagues polemically attacked was the acceptance of such politically ambiguous notions as mobility and network as the fundamental diagram of the city, and at the same time the appropriation of such socially regressive models as the neighborhood, the village, and the community as idealized and falsified representations of the city. In this sense, the group wrote, "The present historical condition of the decadence of the bourgeois pattern of settlement, its emergence out of the obscurity of premodern civilization with its rural, picturesque imagery into a generic economic dynamism, appears to constitute the very form of the urban project and its current paralysis."[91]

The most symptomatic evidence of this paralysis was the

megastructure, widely embraced at this date as a new scale of urban intervention. In the view of Rossi and his colleagues, the exemplary case was Kenzo Tange's project for Tokyo Bay. Based strictly on traffic patterns of distribution and access and completely isolated in Tokyo Bay, the city designed by Tange and his collaborators in 1960 was an immense plug-in diagram of urban capsules structured by functional and technical relationships. In this technologically advanced mode of designing the city, the Venice Group saw the emergence of a politically regressive model: "it still uses the old theme of functionalism while exaggerating [the new] technologies as its urban *raison d'être;* it does not propose any real alternative to the current way of living in the capitalist city."[92]

For Rossi and his colleagues, therefore, the city's technological advancement coincided with its political decadence. In this sense, there was more than an incidental analogy between Rossi's idea of autonomy and the Autonomist positions of Panzieri and Tronti. All were attempts to demystify capitalist development by opposing to the continuity of economic development the separateness of both society and the city. These formulations challenged the primacy of economic determinants over political action. To the tendentious abstractions of economic programming and capitalist planning, Rossi, like Panzieri and Tronti, counterposed a reality based on the tension between antagonists. For the Operaists, this conflict played out in the political and institutional forms that the working class evolved out of its own experience; for Rossi and his colleagues, it played out in the form of the individuality of the urban artifact, the singularity of the *locus,* and the idea of the city of separate parts.

Fully exemplary of Rossi's position was the manifesto-project that he presented together with Luca Meda and Gianugo Polesello at the competition for the new *centro direzionale* (administrative center) of Turin in 1962. The competition was a characteristic effort by Italian industrial cities like Turin and Milan to modernize by taking into account the increasing importance of the white-collar and service sector. The competition was held at the same time as the protest of Piazza Statuto, discussed earlier, and it thus took place amid a social and political transformation of the city's work force. It was the intention of the organizers that the *centro direzionale* become the symbol of a new condition of work completely emancipated from the traditional places of production. Moreover, the competition, which saw massive participation by the most representative architecture offices in Italy, was interpreted by many as a paradigmatic test case for the themes of the new urban dimension and the city-territory. The challenge for many participants seems to have been to find an adequate architectural language to express phenomena that went well beyond architecture, including developments in planning, communications, information exchange, and the use of new technologies, taken together as signifying a radical renewal of the relationship between labor and the city. It is therefore not surprising that many of the entries—including the one submitted by the studio AUA, led by Tafuri and Piccinato—translated the theme of the new urban dimension, with all its cultural and technological values, into megastructural, organicist, and open-work forms.

Against this scenario, Rossi, Meda, and Polesello presented the austere and closed forms of a monumental square building with an internal court. It dialectically counterposed itself as an alter ego to Alessandro Antonelli's Mole, the colossal synagogue in the center of Turin built in the second half of the nineteenth century. Although both structures presented themselves as monumental exceptions within the city, the square form of the Mole Antonelliana and the court building of Rossi, Meda, and Polesello were actually nothing but extrusions of the chessboard grid that constitutes the Roman plan of Turin. But while Antonelli's Mole relates directly to this grid, the Rossi project, located (by the competition) on a site on the periphery 26, 27 of the city, was an analogous reconstruction—in other words, the grid reinterpreted as a typological theme. It was thus not the rehabilitation of a norm, but an analogical use of the norm as a form of exception. Contrary to the other projects presented in the competition, virtually all inspired by the technological novelties of Turin's modernizing infrastructure, it staged a critical and dialectical confrontation with the existing city. Refusing to be an infrastructural scheme, it projected instead a precisely defined *locus*, which, by virtue of its form and location, sharply contrasted and conflicted with the other parts of the city. The city's development was thus represented not as a totalizing image but as a clear form that both constituted and limited the advancing urban development. It was for this reason that the project was immediately rejected by the jury as "reactionary architecture" and labeled "a Stalinist court for mass execution."[93] Its hard-core character, which proposed to offer a civic reference within the city that exposed the new geography of Turin's labor force, was condemned by those who represented the dominant class interests. They preferred to conceal their power behind the rhetoric of a *centro direzionale* that purported to be an efficient, futuristic Eden of labor.

For Rossi, on the other hand, the project in its austere civic character was not so much intended as an architecture of resistance as one of power, which nonetheless, by adopting this position, left open space for its counterparts in the city. The idea of the city of conflicting parts was thus indirectly but implicitly expressed in the project. Architecture for Rossi could not fail to be an expression of the power of the dominant class, but in making decisions for the city, the dominant class could not do other than position itself with respect to the forces antagonistic to it. Rossi's project proposed to be a new civic monument, one that by virtue of its strong critical presence immediately referred to its adversary. Yet while the dominant class sought to evade political responsibility for its role within the development of the capitalist city, Rossi sought to reveal this role, making explicit that all buildings in the city were inevitably representations of power: "There are no buildings of opposition," Rossi wrote, "because the architecture *that is going to be realized* is always an expression of the dominant class."[94] Consequently, it was necessary for the project to exhibit through its own formal devices an argument with respect to power. Only on the basis of such a clear formal proposal was political choice possible, that is, for the community "to decide collectively in favor of one kind of city and to reject another one."[95]

This was the framework within which originated the austere and simple formal language that was to characterize the rationalist project of Rossi in the years ahead. Instead of using novel styles and images that could be consumed along with the new technologies, Rossi opted for a rigid grammar of forms. These forms did not aspire to be anything else but themselves. They thus shifted attention to the *locus* as a symbolic and geographic singularity, a state of exception within the city, posing a challenge to the open-ended space of the capitalist city-territory. Analogous to Tronti's autonomy of the political, which was an inquiry directed not at the autonomy of one part of society with respect to another but at the autonomy of power itself, Rossi's autonomy of architecture was above all about the establishment of urban concepts that posited the supremacy of politics over the city's accelerating economic development.

Archizoom: The Autonomy of Theory versus the Ideology of the Metropolis

In 1965 the same Operaist militant Claudio Greppi who had been one of the authors of a critique of the city-territory in Quaderni rossi two years earlier presented a provocational diploma project [35, 36] at the school of architecture in Florence. It consisted of an urban design for the Piana di Firenze, a vast region between the cities of Florence and Prato, which at that time was emerging as the most important industrial textile region in Italy. In Greppi's project the Piana di Firenze was envisioned as a gigantic factory.[96] He conceived it as an urban application of Tronti's theory of society as a factory, which, as we have seen, extended the idea of production beyond the factory to social relations.

The process of capitalist integration had engendered the disappearance of the proletariat as a group clustered around the productive centers and had had the effect of proletarianizing the entirety of society. This transformation had affected all aspects of life, including the human habitat and, according to Greppi, radically changed the geography of work in the city. The idea of the urban center as a place of financial accumulation and the periphery as a place of production was increasingly superseded by a model in which production and accumulation coincided within an ever expanding, ever more isotropic plan. This isotropic plan was imagined by Greppi as finally liberated from bourgeois ideological representations of the city in their various traditional figurative and spatial forms. Instead, it prepared for an "ultimate" clash between, on the one hand, the workers and, on the other, capitalism, implicating the entire urban infrastructure—the city itself.

In his project, Greppi interpreted the Piana di Firenze as a microcosm of the contemporary process of urban transformation. In the face of this process Greppi saw the only conceivable project as *a theory of the city* and, as its radical consequence, an appropriation of this theory by the workers. Greppi's project was thus not so much a denunciation of capitalist exploitation of the urban territory as a plan that conceived the workers as potentially taking control of it. For Greppi, the Piana di Firenze represented a diffuse and sophisticated system of territorial exploitation that, theorized in militant terms, could become a counterproject: the city of contemporary workers, the place where workers would acquire consciousness of their decisive political power.

Greppi's project, which clearly reflects his critique of the concept of the city-territory, appeared one year before the formation of the Archizoom group. Archizoom was made up of Andrea Branzi, Gilberto Corretti, Paolo Deganello, and Massimo Morozzi, who were at the time graduates of the same school of architecture; they would be joined in 1968 by the industrial designers Dario and Lucia Bartolini. It is my view that Greppi's student project was a primary impetus for Archizoom's scheme for No-Stop City.[97] In those years Greppi was circulating Friedrich Engels's tract "The Housing Question" among the students in Florence.[98] The thesis of Marx's collaborator was that there is no such thing as a working-class metropolis, only a working-class critique of the existing metropolis. This thesis was taken up by the students to combat the naive illusion that the bourgeois city could be reformed and ameliorated democratically. Against this illusion, radical leftists like Greppi and the members of Archizoom chose to produce neither a project for an alternative city nor even a critique of the existing one, but rather a theory—the theory of the city's development into the ascendant capitalist form of urbanity. According to their analysis, the only way to oppose such a theory to the status quo as a radical critique was to avoid the compromise tactics

37

38

of the capitalist apologists and liberal reformers alike and to embrace the point of view of the workers. The theory of the city, they believed, should project the possibility of the city's appropriation by the workers. It should break with the ideology of the "equilibrium of opposites" that was put forward by capitalist reformers and that was at the heart of the bourgeoisie's power over capitalist development. Presenting its theory for No-Stop City in the pages of Casabella with the title "Città, catena di montaggio del sociale: Ideologia e teoria della metropoli" (City, assembly line of social issues: Ideology and theory of the metropolis), Archizoom explained its critical objective as follows:

> The modern city is born out of capitalism and develops within its logic: capital dictates to the city its general ideology, and this in turn conditions its development and configuration. This general ideology consists of the policy of the "balance of opposites," pursued in relation to economic demands and "produced de facto" in relation to the plan of urban operation.... What is vital to say first and foremost is that the working-class metropolis does not exist. The birth of the modern capitalist city does not make it possible for the city actually to enjoy autonomous political growth (something possible for the working class itself), but merely to acquire features which, once ideological mystifications have been left behind, permit a scientific development of the debate. What is thus involved is a theory and not an alternative proposition. Just as there is no class-based political economy, so there can only be a class critique of urbanism. To carry forward this endeavor, we have used a classic written language along with a graphic language that is more specific to our discipline.[99]

Made up of architects and designers whose practice in the 1970s and 1980s would especially be in the field of industrial design, the Archizoom group began by aspiring to be a critical and sarcastic "parody" of the British collective Archigram.[100] But if for Archigram technology was a culturally progressive and politically neutral creative device through which to design the iconography of a brave new world, for Archizoom the application of innovative technology to the territory meant a theoretical interrogation of the form of the capitalist city. As embodied in their work, the task of architecture was not an iconic rendering of the city's industrial development, but rather the demystification of urban ideology by means of an autonomous theory that lucidly explained the city's dissolution as a consequence of the historical development of capitalism.

It is in this sense that Branzi may be said to have pushed to its extreme consequences Rossi's embrace of theory as the role of the architecture project, on the one hand, and Tronti's idea of *sichtbar machen*—making things visible—on the other. Making things visible meant opposing to ideology (which for Tronti was always bourgeois ideology) a theory that would render in objective terms the spatial relationships established by capitalist production. Thus, for Branzi and Archizoom, the project of autonomy was not autonomy of architectural form, but rather the potential autonomy of theory from the mystifications inherited from the capitalist development of the city. To the consoling and compensatory forms of the bourgeois city as reflected in its historical manifestations, Archizoom sought to oppose a deliberately cynical realism concerning the diabolical forces of capitalism, and to posit the idea that, if objectively represented, they might become an actual weapon by which the working class could take possession and power. Such a project would assume the form of new "wild realities," as they put it, inserted at the point of capitalism's most advanced development.

No-Stop City was thus intended by Archizoom—at least in the early stages—to be a theoretical test of the possibility of wild realities emerging within a city conceived as a unique and endless interior wherein all functions of inhabitation were pushed to their most extreme technological development. Archizoom explained the coincidence between advanced technological development and the untamed human nature growing within it in language that seems to have come directly out of Tronti's political theory of the working class as a negative trigger of development:

> These "wild" realities represent each time a leap forward and, at the same time, the obscure intent of a foreign body within a rational mechanism. The greatest of these wild realities, or rather their sum, is thus the working class, which comes into being under capitalism as labor power, but which actually represents its alternative.[101]

For Archizoom, then, the alternative to the capitalist city was the city's potential alternative use by its own producers, that is, by its working class. It was for this reason that the city had to be theorized in terms of its most advanced stage of development—i.e., *ad absurdum*, in its extreme consequences, to the point that these consequences were not controllable even by the system itself. "It is only in this way, by making the brain of the system mad, that we can interrupt the continuity of the [capitalist] process and the entirety of its links."[102] Archizoom's theoretical scheme thus followed closely the one elaborated by Tronti with respect to the working-class struggle, the main principle of which was, as we have seen, not to resolve the contradiction between the workers and the system of production, but to exploit it. In order to do so, the workers had to exasperate the system to the point of a final political explosion in the form of the workers' taking of power.

For this reason No-Stop City should be read as an architecture stripped of all qualities and reduced to a rigorous representation of the system prepared for a new use. The project consisted of a series of drawings and texts presented in the form of an instruction manual. If the text allowed Archizoom to offer a series of cogent hypotheses on the use of the city, the drawings emphasized the autonomous and disciplinary nature of the critique. The plans, sections, diagrams, perspectives, and models depict a minimal urban environment homogenized by its infrastructural system. The initial drawing is a typed grid of dots that represents the basic organizational scheme for the supporting structure and the energy plug-ins. The representation simplifies the technocratic power of capitalism into the simplest possible "nonfigurative" schema, polemically rejecting the iconic exuberance through which architecture has historically tended to incarnate technology.

According to Archizoom, the city *was* what it *did:* it was nothing but its own (re)productive system reduced to an architectural degree zero: air-conditioned space and "a bathroom every 50 meters." This meant that the city was simply the precondition for the reproduction of a labor force stripped of any mystifications that were capable of concealing its ideological premises. The project's polemical intent was perfectly clear:

in contrast to the celebratory graphics of Archigram and the technocratic futurism of the Japanese Metabolists, Archizoom proposed a city *ohne Eigenschaften*, without qualities, cold, neoclassical, without architecture because it itself was nothing but an immense, endless architecture. Its archetype for Archizoom was neither the traditional form of production (the factory) nor the traditional form of consumption (housing), but the coincidence of the two in a single urban function: parking, storage, shopping—the supermarket. In Archizoom's words:

> The only place where the factory model and the consumption model come together is the supermarket. This is the real yardstick and model of the future city and, consequently, of reality as a whole: homogeneous utopian structure, private functionality, rational sublimation of consumption. Maximum result for minimum effort. The supermarket foreshadows an image-free structure, but one which offers an optimum system of information for goods and merchandise, within which the homogeneity of the product is directly produced. As a homogeneous amalgam of all real data there is no longer any need for "zoning." The supermarket becomes an experimental field in which different cultures of the "soil" are actually exceeded: urban culture and agricultural culture. Elevations are formed in the supermarket just as in agriculture, i.e., by the purely functional accumulation of reality. The "landscape" no longer exists as an external phenomenon since the profound nature of capitalism becomes a formal freedom expressing all its rational potential.[103]

As Branzi himself has often recalled, the stripped-down language of No-Stop City was a radicalization *ad absurdum* of the most rigorously rationalist legacy of modern architecture, the same legacy that at the time was being recuperated by Rossi. Clearly a crucial reference for No-Stop City was the urban research of Hilberseimer, who at this same date was also being rediscovered by Giorgio Grassi, an architect close to Rossi. In 1967, Grassi edited and introduced the Italian translation of Hilberseimer's late book Entfaltung einer Planungsidee (The development of a planning idea).[104] Compared to the picturesque urban utopias of the 1960s, Hilberseimer's *Groszstadtarchitektur* appeared as a project that fully accepted capitalist control over urban reality while demystifying its pretended representations through the radically didactic, "inhuman" simplicity of its

39

architectonic form. What is fascinating about Hilberseimer is the consistency and rigor of his writing, a style far distant from the more propaganda-like pronouncements of such better-known Modern Movement architects as Le Corbusier. Like young Italian architects of the 1960s such as Rossi, Grassi, and Archizoom, Hilberseimer was a prolific writer and a reluctant builder, and there is a striking contrast between the highly sophisticated theory of the city that appears in his writings and the absolute simplicity of his projects.

But if for Rossi and Grassi the obstinate simplicity of Hilberseimer's architecture constituted the reference for a public and civic architecture of the city, for Branzi, on the contrary, the same formal simplicity inspired a form of city that had no value to represent other than its own use-value as a system to be appropriated by the emerging urban proletariat. Hilberseimer's *Groszstadt*, and especially his studies and projects for the American city, were understood by Branzi as representations of a city without architecture, if we mean by architecture the figurative quality of the city, its image. It is for this reason that 33, 34 the representational techniques of Branzi and Archizoom clearly appear to have been inherited from Hilberseimer's black-and-white perspectives of the *Groszstadt* and the repetitive patterns in his projects for the American suburbs. Both Archizoom's and Hilberseimer's cold urban representations paradoxically combine the maximum effort to eliminate any architecturally expressive gesture with an image made only by architectural signs like columns, walls, elevators, and furniture. For Branzi, such signs were the absolute minimum representation of a city liberated from its image, and thus from any recognizable values or civic iconography. As Branzi has recently written about No-Stop City:

The idea of an inexpressive, catatonic architecture, the outcome of the expansive forms of logic of the system and its class antagonisms, was the only modern architecture of interest to us: a liberating architecture, corresponding to mass democracy, devoid of *demos* and of *cratos* (of people and of power), and both centerless and imageless. A society freed from the rhetorical forms of humanitarian socialism and rhetorical progressivism: an architecture that gazed fearlessly at the logic of gray, unaesthetic, and de-dramatized industrialism.... The colorful visions of Pop architecture were replaced by Ludwig

Hilberseimer's pitiless urban images, those of a city without qualities designed for people without preordained qualities—free, therefore, to express in an autonomous way their own creative, political, and behavioral energies. The greatest possible freedom occurred where integration was strongest.... Alienation was a new artistic condition.[105]

It was in this sense that the work of the Archizoom group and its interpretation of autonomy as the liberation and radicalization of a global theoretical outlook on the forms of production of the contemporary city strongly differed from that of other architects and groups of the day like Superstudio, even if the two were subsequently brought together under the promotional label "Radical Architecture." Archizoom and Superstudio began in close cultural and generational proximity, absorbing the same cultural and political context. But while Superstudio was interested in a half-ironic, half-serious rediscovery of silent, ritualistic architectural archetypes as a way of going beyond and through the forms of mass consumption, Archizoom focused on the development of a coherent, at times lyrical, and cynical theory of the metropolis seen as the nihilistic destruction of all values, that is, of all previous urban figures and rituals. If, with the project for a Continuous Monument, Superstudio offered the image of an architecture without a city, Archizoom conversely investigated the preconditions for a city without an architecture.

In this respect, Archizoom's reinterpretation of the objectivism of Hilberseimer came very close to Tafuri's appraisal of the same architect in his Contropiano contribution "Per una critica dell'ideologia architettonica," although with a totally different conclusion. Tafuri's hostility toward the Florentine avant-garde and especially toward Archizoom is well known. However, this hostility appears a bit surprising when one contextualizes both Archizoom's early writings on No-Stop City, as published in Casabella in 1970 and Domus in 1971, and Tafuri's critique of architectural ideology, as published in Contropiano. Not only did the members of Archizoom make reference to Tafuri's essay in their own presentation in Casabella, but both Branzi and Tafuri counterposed the ideology of modern architecture to the formal dissolution of metropolitan space, which in turn led each to a disenchanted theory of the metropolis

40, 41

centered on the system itself rather than its buildings. In commenting on Hilberseimer's theoretical attitude toward the city, Tafuri wrote:

In the face of modernized production techniques and the expansion and rationalization of the market, the architect, as producer of "objects," became an incongruous figure. It was no longer a question of giving form to single elements of the urban fabric, nor even to simple prototypes. Once the true unity of the production cycle has been identified in the city, the only task the architect can have is to *organize* the cycle. Taking this proposition to its extreme conclusion, Hilberseimer insists on the role of elaborating "organizational models" as the only one that can fully reflect the need for Taylorizing building production, as the new task of the technician, who is now completely integrated into this process.

On the basis of this position, Hilberseimer was able to avoid involvement in the "crisis of the object" so anxiously articulated by such architects as Loos and Taut. For Hilberseimer, the object was not in crisis because it had already disappeared from his spectrum of considerations. The only emerging imperative was that dictated by the laws of organization, and therein lies what has been correctly seen as Hilberseimer's greatest contribution.[106]

Thus, what Tafuri insisted was Hilberseimer's greatest contribution was what Archizoom further developed in No-Stop City: the city as a continuous system rather than a collection of objects. Foreshadowing later theories of media and immaterial production, Branzi emphasized that if the city was integrated into the cycle of production, then producing it was only a matter of programming, not of designing, its built structures. However, if the call for programming as an alternative strategy to architecture was eventually—thirty years later—to end up in a vague imaginary of diagrams and statistics, Archizoom's and Tafuri's ideas of programming and organization converged in the formulation of a cohesive and integral critique of the capitalist metropolis.

For both Tafuri and Archizoom, to program and organize urban space to its extreme consequences, as in Hilberseimer's *Groszstadt*, was the only way to achieve an autonomous role not for architects, but for urban and architectural theory. However, the conclusions that Tafuri and Archizoom drew from this position were radically different. For Tafuri, the production cycle was to be understood within the reality of large-scale industry and, although far beyond the expressive power of architecture to represent it, was still controllable through the tools of planning. As we have seen, Tafuri more or less reduced Operaism's "negative thought" to an idea of urban process, which, even if it dissolved the architectural object, still had the potential to be resolved within the dialectics of planning. For Branzi, on the other hand, the extreme objectivity of the production cycle ultimately had irrational effects within the city. These effects were completely uncontrollable in their entirety; only perhaps at the scale of furniture or the "object"—a scale of design that would, in fact, constitute the focus of the members of Archizoom after the conclusion of No-Stop City—could they be modified.

For Tafuri, in other words, the paradigm of production remained that of Fordism, with its contradictions but also with its intelligibility as "planning," while for Archizoom it was clear that the Fordist assembly line was undergoing a process of transformation in which the rationality of the plan was being replaced by a much more decentralized and pervasive system of production and consumption. In this new scenario, where the city was endlessly disposable and consumable, and where its form and organization were consequently less controllable, both architecture and its opposite, planning, were seen by Archizoom as completely inadequate instruments for action. Interior design, on the other hand, offered a way to "embrace" a sprawling urbanism as the new form of the late-capitalist city. If this approach proved to be an anticipation of what indeed happened in the 1980s and '90s, when the role of the designed object overtook that of architecture in shaping the urban scenario, it is precisely for this reason that the "critical" legacy of Archizoom's project of autonomy remains ambiguous. With the defeat of the working class as a political subject in the 1970s, it became increasingly unclear to what extent the scenario of total integration predicted by Archizoom was, in the end, a "natural effect" of the hedonistic, creative, and apolitical destiny of humanity—as Branzi has seemed to suggest recently in his attempt to "soften" the original meaning of the project[107]—or was, alternatively, a "conscious" product of this class as a specific political subject. Indeed, the ambiguity of No-Stop City sums up the many ambiguities that characterized the passage from Operaism to Autonomia, in which, as we have seen, the latter movement seems to have been more invested in reconciling its ideas and strategies with the prevailing trends of a (capitalist) postmodernism than in defining a clear, antagonistic alternative to it.

Aftermath

In spite of the weaknesses and contradictions that emerged, which would become increasingly clear in the course of their historical evolution, all the projects I have described in the preceding pages were clearly conceived by their authors as attempts to construct a new political subject. This subject was intended to replace the institutions of capitalism and even those of liberal democracy while acting at the same scale and with the same degree of power. In the 1970s, however, capitalism's restructuring as a consequence of precisely that development which the Operaists were theorizing in the 1960s—the workers' struggle against the Fordist and Taylorist system of production—pushed not only the new post-Fordist modes of production, but also all the political institutions in Italy, toward an irreversible crisis of representation and militancy that affected even those who were contesting those institutions. The crisis took the form of an intense polarization between public institutions like parties, unions, and official cultural organizations, on the one hand, and politically radical groups, on the other. If the intellectual's project of autonomy in the 1960s had been founded with the objective of challenging those institutions by eventually taking power over them, in the 1970s this challenge was not just exacerbated but exasperated as it became—as Branzi has recently stated—"a conflict within the Left."[108]

  The result of this conflict was to push politics in two opposing directions: toward a blind, at times delirious, and self-destructive critique of all institutions and organizations, and toward the comfortable spaces of academia, the institution *par excellence*. It was the growing relevance of the latter, seen as a new site of contestation replacing the factory, that was to attract many intellectuals away from the front lines of the workers' struggle and the politics of workers' institutions. A fundamental point of no return in the war occurring within the Left was May 1968. What had been imagined and dreamed of by many leftist intellectuals as a political revolution of the working class suddenly took the unprecedented form of a "student revolution." Unlike in France, the protests of 1968 in Italy were inseparable from the "hot autumn" of 1969, which was a true "workers' struggle." However, this struggle soon saw the rise of a new generation of protesters formed out of the burgeoning middle class, brought up on fashionable cultural critiques especially imported from France.

Throughout the 1960s all the protagonists of the cultural project of autonomy had used theory as a strategic preparation for the new role that their disciplines were to play in the public arena. Like politics, poetics were theorized as a vital instrument of social transformation. This led to the interesting paradox that the intense debate fostered by the project of autonomy crossed disciplinary lines. Such a situation occurred because of the urgency of constructing a new subject able to comprehend the new forms of economic and cultural power at the deepest level. However, if the 1960s were characterized by a messianic expectation of a new revolutionary subject, the 1970s was a period in which many militants discovered that revolutions in the affluent countries of Western Europe could only take the form of isolated revolts. If this reality pushed militant creativity toward innovative but less politicized forms of struggle, it left unchallenged the whole political class dominating the ruling institutions, whose cultural and ideological devolution in Italy in the 1980s and the 1990s reached the lowest point in the country's political and cultural history since the Renaissance. What arose within this desolate scenario of the collapse and confusion of the political—which today, in the current wave of 1970s revivalism, tends to be romanticized as the beginning of new forms of "postpolitics"—was a radicalism without any urgency. This is exemplified by the post-Operaist Autonomia's ingenious transformation of politics into an enthusiastic celebration of a postmodernity viewed as a cultural liberation from the older forms of workers' struggle.

80

It was, however, with the loss of urgency in the 1970s and 1980s of the demand for autonomy and decision-making power that the respective disciplines, from politics and philosophy to architecture and urbanism, fell into specialized disciplinary slots and became autonomous not with respect to contemporary political-economic reality but simply with respect to one another. Equally ironic, it was within this scenario that the celebration and global exportation of Italian autonomy took place, to the point that we can say that the international triumph of the project occurred at the moment of its internal collapse.[109]

As is well known, the success of Italian architecture internationally—especially in the United States—coincided with two major "museum" events: the Fifteenth Triennale in   42, 43 Milan, curated by Aldo Rossi in 1973, and the Museum of Modern Art exhibition "Italy: The New Domestic Landscape," curated by Emilio Ambasz in 1972. In the first, Rossi extended the project of autonomy to other international groups and movements that did not share his own political motivations. In the second, Ambasz celebrated the innovative aesthetic style of "radical architecture" rather than its political background. Moreover, the label "radical" as used by many critics and thinkers to refer to movements in architecture, art, design, and politics during the 1970s was directly at odds with the intentions of many protagonists of these movements. Superstudio's cofounder Cristiano Toraldo di Francia has said recently that when the art critic Germano Celant invented the label *Architettura Radicale* (rendered in English as *Radical Design*) in 1972, both Superstudio and Archizoom realized that their project had come to an end.[110] Commodified in the pages of the architecture magazines as another avant-garde gesture, it was no longer an attempt to criticize the existing forms of theoretical and building production.[111] This self-assessment comes very close to Tronti's skepticism toward the "radical politics" of the Autonomia groups of the 1970s; according to Tronti, the adjective *radical* before the word *politics* meant that the politics could no longer stand alone.

It is thus ironic that these two major exhibitions, the Triennale and the MoMA show, were internationally received as the seminal events of, respectively, "autonomous architecture" and "radical architecture." Rather than inaugurating new theoretical positions, in fact, these events coincided with the very end of the two movements in Italy. By the beginning of the 1970s the theories that were initially conceived as contributions to the political and social struggles of the city became mired in the discourse of academia and the space of exhibitions, where critics and curators adapted them to the cultural fashion of the moment. The rather melancholic Rossian imagery of autonomous architecture, seen as detached from the increasing complexity of the city, and conversely, the avant-garde imagery of radical architecture, seen as a celebration of the expanding space of information, were both a *posteriori* products of export lacking in any political frame. The related formation of "schools" and the extreme professionalization of knowledge, both of which had already been foreseen by the Operaists, quickly dissolved any hope of real—that is, political—autonomy.

The main damage suffered by these theories, however, occurred when both the politics and the poetics of autonomy were read as emblems of an ascendant "postmodernism" rather than as the finale of the modern conception of politics and poetics within and against capitalism. What, then, is the utility of looking back at this project? Why return to this intense period of theoretical reflection that has, in the end, produced so little of consequence, especially in the country where it originated? As an Italian architect working mostly outside of Italy today, I find it fascinating and at the same time exhilarating that those from abroad consider this legacy interesting and appealing, while in Italy it is not only neglected but even despised, and not always for wrong reasons. If outside of Italy the reference to "autonomia" evokes cutting-edge politics, inside it is still associated with the political disarming of the Left and the general depoliticization of postmodern society.

In this essay I have attempted to tell the story of "how it happened," avoiding both revivalist celebration but also peremptory rejection. There is no doubt that my effort has been motivated by a deep feeling of affinity toward the various protagonists of the autonomy project. But it is by looking at these figures retrospectively, through the experience of their failures, which coincided with my own formation during the 1990s, that it is finally possible to dispel nostalgia for history and consider what might be recuperated from this legacy. I believe it is possible to learn from these experiences how a new political subject might be materially constructed from within, but ideologically against, the very constraints of our civilization—a civilization that, in spite of its ongoing transformations, remains a civilization of labor.

By excavating history more deeply, by going beyond the clichés of activism, and by eschewing the postmodern appropriations of "radicalism," one may grasp what is still vital in the legacy of autonomy: namely that it was one of the most rigorous efforts ever attempted to theorize a grand narrative of the political, challenging the very premises of capitalism (as well as its contemporary avatar, "Empire"). In a time when an army of theorists occupying the seats of academia is obsessed with the idea of "practice" and pays lip service to "activism" as the only valid space for cultural, social, and political action, the project of autonomy reminds us that the most challenging efforts within and against capitalism are those born out of "Theory" with a capital T—Theory, that is, not as a device aimed simply at reporting on the "reality as found" of the city and its changes every Monday morning, but as a way to establish long-term responsibilities and solid categories by which to counter the positivistic and mystifying ways that social and political development comes to be seen as evolutionary progress. It is as a theoretical project—as a project made of the "patience of research and the urgency of the answer"[112]—that the project of autonomy may be seen as relevant less in terms of its specific content, and more so as a lesson in method on how the most challenging theoretical effort might become the most effective form of "practicing" struggle.

Notes

This small book originated from the many discussions I had with Joan Ockman over the course of two years of collaboration on the FORuM Project at the Buell Center at Columbia University. Joan not only served as an incisive editor of this essay, but she helped inspire its argument concerning the relevance of form as a "strategy" for understanding architecture's relationship to the city and politics. I wish to express my deep appreciation to her for both her intellectual comradeship and the hospitality that she provided to me under the auspices of the Buell Center. I would also like to thank Sara Goldsmith of the Buell Center for her professional stewardship of this book's production. While writing this essay I had the opportunity to discuss its main thesis and my thoughts about the legacy of Operaism with Mario Tronti. I am enormously grateful to him for his intellectual generosity and for supporting the project of writing this essay. I hope this book will serve to make more widely known the thought of someone whom I believe is one of the greatest thinkers of the last forty years. Finally, I would like to dedicate this book to Luigi, Lucia, Annalisa, and Alice. — P.V.A.

1. Cornelius Castoriadis, "The Retreat from Autonomy: Postmodernism as Generalized Conformism," in The World in Fragments (Stanford, CA: Stanford University Press, 1997), p. 32.
2. Ibid., p. 41.
3. Ibid.
4. Ibid., p. 34.
5. Ibid., p. 38.
6. Ibid., p. 42.
7. These are the words Sylvère Lotringer uses to introduce the forthcoming new edition of the issue on Autonomia that he edited for Semiotext(e) in 1980. See Sylvère Lotringer and Christian Marazzi, eds., Autonomia, Post-Political Politics (Cambridge, MA: MIT Press, 2007).
8. The story of Operaism can be summarized in the publication of three fundamental journals that span the decade 1961–71. These journals are Quaderni rossi (1961–65), Classe operaia (1964–66), and finally Contropiano (1968–71). In 1972 Mario Tronti delivered a seminar on the notion of political autonomy, published five years later under the title "L'autonomia del politico." In my view, it is precisely the argument of the autonomy of the political from economic determination—as presented by Tronti in 1972—that is the core and essence of Operaism. For the most detailed and precise reconstruction of the history of Operaism, especially the transition from Quaderni rossi to Classe operaia, see the interview with Rita di Leo in Giuseppe Trotta, ed., "Per una storia di Classe operaia," in Bailamme 24/2 (1999), pp. 173–205.
9. The story of the evolution from "Operaismo" to "Autonomia Operaia" (subsequently simply known as "Autonomia") is complex and dramatic. It involves differences, divisions, splits, and collapses among the many protagonists of these movements. The history of these movements can be very roughly divided into three main chapters. While often superficially lumped together under the term "Autonomia," these chapters actually correspond to three radically different moments: Operaism (early 1960s–1968); Potere Operaio (Workers' Power, 1967–1973); and Autonomia Operaia (Workers Autonomy, 1976–1978). The first movement was characterized by intense theoretical production; the second by a radical but less original elaboration of the premises of the first, especially reflecting Negri's post-Communist position; the third by militancy over theoretical speculation. Despite the many protagonists, there is no doubt that only three fundamental figures provided the movement's originality. These were Raniero Panzieri (1921–64), who may be considered the progenitor of Operaism; Mario Tronti (1931–), who has been the main theorist of Operaism; and finally Antonio (Toni) Negri (1933–), whose ideas were formed under both Panzieri and Tronti, and who later become the main reference for Potere Operai as well as the Autonomia groups. It is interesting to note that on the history of Operaism and Autonomia there are more sources available in English than in Italian, with many of the English-language sources on the Internet. However, some of these are very imprecise, suffering from lack of access to the original material and to the individuals involved. Of the three movements, the one that has suffered most from a lack of precise consideration—Operaism—is the movement that has provided the whole development with its most original ideas. This is partly because of the extreme rigor and absence of intellectual narcissism in its theoretical style, which does not really fit into the "creative" interpretation of Autonomia, and partly because its protagonists—especially Panzieri and Tronti—had little interest in promoting their theories outside the context of political militancy. Conversely, Negri has been always keen to cultivate his position in academia both in Italy and in France. For a reliable history of Operaism and Autonomia in English, see Steve Wright, Storming Heaven: Class Composition and Struggle in Italian Autonomist Marxism (London: Pluto Press, 2002).
10. See Mario Tronti, L'autonomia del politico (Milan: Feltrinelli, 1977).
11. Mario Tronti, interview, in Guido Borio, Francesca Pozzi, and Gigi Roggero, eds., Gli operaisti (Rome: Derive a Approdi, 2005), p. 281.
12. Again, in distinction to its reputation outside of Italy, "Scuola di Venezia" refers specifically to a period at the IUAV when, within the program directed by Aymonino, the theories of Rossi were dominant. Aymonino was invited to teach at the IUAV by Samonà in 1963 and Rossi applied to be his assistant. The class taught by Aymonino and Rossi through 1965 produced two small booklets on the relationship between typology and morphology, and these became the Scuola di Venezia's methodological incunabula. Rossi and Aymonino were quickly joined by young assistant professors in

the IUAV like Costantino Dardi, Gianugo Polesello, Emilio Mattioni, and Luciano Semerani. Semerani and Polesello were, like Rossi, regular contributors to Rogers's Casabella. On the formation of this group, see, Claudia Conforti's interview with Aymonino in Claudia Conforti, Carlo Aymonino: L'architettura non è un mito (Rome: Officina, 1980), p. 174. The main hypotheses of this Venice group were later developed in an important book on the city of Padua published by the Communist publishing house Officina. See Carlo Aymonino, Manlio Brusatin, Gianni Fabbri, Mauro Lena, Pasquale Lovero, Sergio Lucianetti, and Aldo Rossi, La città di Padova: Saggio di analisi urbana (Rome: Officina, 1970).
13. The Gruppo Architettura comprised professors at the IUAV who gathered around Aymonino between 1968 and 1974 after Aymonino replaced Samonà as director of the school. However, the group's main hypotheses—notably the interpretation and design of the city in terms of the relationship between morphology and typology—were the same as Rossi and Aymonino had already elaborated in 1963–65. On the Gruppo Architettura, see Carlo Aymonino, Costantino Dardi, Gianni Fabbri, Raffaele Panella, Gianugo Polesello, and Luciano Semerani, Per un'idea di città: La ricerca del Gruppo Architettura a Venezia (1968–1974) (Venice: Cluva, 1984).
14. The main protagonists of what later would be called "Architettura Radicale" by the Italian art critics were Andrea Branzi, Gilberto Corretti, and Massimo Morozzi, who would form the group Archizoom, and Adolfo Natalini and Cristiano Toraldo di Francia, who would form the group Superstudio. Corretti and Morozzi of Archizoom and Toraldo di Francia of Superstudio were the most politicized members of the respective groups, and they were in direct contact with members of the Florentine section of the Operaists. The best-known members of both groups, Andrea Branzi and Adolfo Natalini, with whom the identity of these groups is often associated, were less involved in the "political" content of Archizoom's and Superstudio's work. In a lecture at the Berlage Institute in Rotterdam in 2007, Toraldo di Francia recalled his "friendly divergence" from his comrade Natalini, who at the time was a member of Gioventù Liberale (Liberal Youth), a Center-Right student movement. A similar divergence occurred within Archizoom, where Morozzi and Corretti's political extremism was often at odds with Branzi's more moderate position. On the so-called radical architecture groups in Florence, there is a vast literature that tends to be either uncritically apologetic or else superficially negative. A common trait of this literature is the stubborn removal of the work of Archizoom and Superstudio from their respective political contexts, the latter usually being reduced to the liberative climax of the protests of 1968. No publication mentions the direct relationship between the theories of these groups and the political themes developed by Operaism, including the "refusal of work" that both practiced by resisting being absorbed into traditional forms of professional practice and elaborating alternatives to it.
15. The early group of Operaists was made up of young intellectuals who gathered around Panzieri and came mainly from Rome, Turin, Milan, and Mestre. The members from Rome, including Mario Tronti and Alberto Asor Rosa, were considered the "theorists." The Turinese and Milanese members, including Vittorio Reiser and Romano Alquati, were known as the "sociologists" since they were primarily interested in undertaking social research focused on FIAT in Turin and Olivetti in Ivrea. The Mestre members, including Antonio Negri, were interested in applying theoretical work on militancy within the factory, specifically the chemical factory at Porto Marghera. For a reconstruction of the different positions within the Operaist group, see Borio et al., Gli operaisti.
16. Adolf Berle as quoted by Raniero Panzieri, in "Relazione sul neocapitalismo," in La ripresa del Marxismo-Leninismo in Italia (Milan: Sapere Edizioni, 1972), p. 178.
17. Ibid. Translations from Italian throughout this essay are my own unless otherwise indicated.
18. See Daniele Balicco, Non parlo a tutti: Franco Fortini intellettuale politico (Rome: Manifesto Libri, 2006), p. 22.
19. This dichotomy would be specifically associated with the thought of the German political theorist Carl Schmitt. It was in the context of an understanding of conflict and struggle as the core of political activism that many leftist intellectuals in the 1970s rediscovered the writings of Schmitt and his conception of the political as based on a determination of who is friend and who is enemy. See Carl Schmitt, The Concept of the Political (Chicago: University of Chicago Press, 1996).
20. Franco Fortini, "Lettera ad amici di Piacenza," in L'ospite ingrato: Testi e note per versi ironici (Bari: De Donato, 1966), pp. 89–97.
21. It is possible to discern a significant difference between the ideology of the group and the currently popular ideology of the network. The group makes of its communal autonomy a one-sided political challenge to the process of integration implicit in the existing forms of the social order. The network, a form of association has been embraced by many contemporary intellectuals, takes the social order for granted—that is, assumes it as a politically neutral device—while regarding the intense dynamism of its technological and communicative apparatus as constituting the deepest form of social order.
22. Raniero Panzieri, "Sull'uso delle macchine nel neocapitalismo," in Quaderni rossi 1 (1961), pp. 53–72.
23. Ibid., p. 59.
24. Ibid., p. 61.
25. Ibid.
26. Ibid., p. 62.
27. Raniero Panzieri, "Relazione sul neocapitalismo," in La Ripresa del Marxismo-Leninismo in Italia, p. 171.
28. On the Olivetti town at Ivrea, see Patrizia Bonifazio, Olivetti costruisce: Architettura moderna a Ivrea (Milan: Skira, 2006).

29. Ibid., p. 195.
30. Theodor W. Adorno, Minima Moralia: Reflections from Damaged Life, trans. E. F. N. Jephcott (London: Verso, 1978), p. 15.
31. Panzieri, "Relazione sul neocapitalismo," p. 212 (my italics).
32. Raniero Panzieri, "Plusvalore e pianificazione: Appunti di lettura del capitale," in Quaderni rossi 4 (1963), pp. 257–77.
33. Ibid., p. 263.
34. Raniero Panzieri, "Sul controllo operaio," in La ripresa del Marxismo-Leninismo in Italia, p. 107.
35. "Il piano del capitale" was originally published |in Quaderni rossi 2 (1963), pp. 44–73. Reprinted in Mario Tronti, Operai e capitale (Turin: Einaudi, 1966), pp. 60–85.
36. Ibid., p. 66.
37. "Lenin in Inghilterra" was originally published in Classe operaia 1 (1964), pp. 1, 18–20; reprinted in Operai e capitale, pp. 89–95.
38. Ibid., p. 89.
39. Mario Tronti, "La fabbrica e la società," originally published in Quaderni rossi 2 (1962), pp. 1–31; reprinted in Operai e capitale, pp. 39–59.
40. Ibid., p. 39.
41. Ibid.
42. Ibid.
43. Ibid., p. 51.
44. Ibid., p. 53.
45. Ibid., p. 47.
46. Ibid.
47. Mario Tronti, "Forza-lavoro classe operaia," in Operai e capitale, p. 128. Tronti's italics.
48. Ibid., p. 127.
49. Ibid., p. 128.
50. Ibid., p. 245.
51. Ibid., p. 242.
52. Ibid., p. 262.
53. Mario Tronti, Sull'autonomia del politico (Milan: Feltrinelli, 1977), p. 16. The seminar was held in December 1972.
54. Tronti, La politica al tramonto (Turin: Einaudi, 1996), p. 159.
55. Tronti, Sull'autonomia del politico, p. 9. Tronti's italics.
56. Tronti, Operai e capitale, p. 269.
57. Mario Tronti, "Il partito come problema," in Contropiano 2 (1968), pp. 299–301.
58. Antonio Negri, "Operai senza alleati," in Classe operaia 3 (1964), pp. 1 and 18.
59. Tronti, Operai e capitale, pp. 96–102.
60. Interview with Mario Tronti, August 2000, in Borio et al., Gli operaisti, p. 300. Tronti emphasizes that he decided to close down Classe operaia after only two years because he realized that the militants in the group were acting as marginal "extremists" rather than rooting their radicalism within the more difficult but necessary ground of the institutionally established political organizations.
61. Massimo Cacciari, "Sulla genesi del pensiero negativo," in Contropiano 1 (1969), pp. 131–201.
62. Ibid., p. 136.
63. Ibid., p. 183.
64. Mario Tronti, "Estremisti e riformisti," in Contropiano 1 (1968), p. 20.
65. Manfredo Tafuri, "Per una critica dell'ideologia architettonica," in Contropiano 1 (1969), pp. 31–79; translated by Stephen Sartorelli as "Toward a Critique of Architectural Ideology," in K. Michael Hays, ed., Architecture Theory since 1968 (Cambridge, MA: MIT Press, 1998), pp. 6–35.
66. Ibid., Contropiano 1, p. 39.
67. Manfredo Tafuri, "Austromarxismo e città: 'Das rote Wien,'" in Contropiano 2 (1971), pp. 257–312.
68. Ibid., p. 263.
69. As stated in a telephone conversation with the author, September 2007.
70. The most important written contributions to the Italian theoretical debate on architecture and the city before the 1960s are the following: Bruno Zevi, Saper vedere l'architettura: Saggio sull'interpretazione spaziale dell'architettura (Turin: Einaudi, 1948); Giulio Carlo Argan, Walter Gropius e la Bauhaus (Turin: Einaudi, 1951); and Ernesto Nathan Rogers, Esperienza dell'architettura (Turin: Einaudi, 1958).
71. Tronti, Operai e capitale, p. 303: "Sichtbar machen means to make visible: to say clearly so as to be understood, even at the risk of not interpreting very well things that are intrinsically obscure."
72. Published as "Architettura per i musei," in Guido Canella et al., Teoria della progettazione architettonica (Bari: Edizioni Dedalo, 1968), p. 123.
73. On the political formation of Aldo Rossi and his relationship with Communist culture, see Pier Vittorio Aureli, "The Difficult Whole: Typology and Singularity of the Urban Event in Aldo Rossi's Early Work, 1954–1963," in Log 9 (2007), pp. 20–41.
74. Carlo Aymonino, Il significato della città (Padua: Marsilio, 2000), p. 4.
75. Aldo Rossi, "Il concetto di tradizione nel neoclassicismo milanese," Società 3 (1956). Reprinted in Rossi, Scritti scelti sull'architettura e la città (Milan: Città Studi Edizioni, 1975), pp. 1–24.
76. See Ezio Bonfanti et al., Architettura razionale (Milan: Franco Angeli, 1973).
77. Aldo Rossi, Introduction, in Bonfanti et al., Architettura razionale, p. 16.
78. Tendenza is a Gramscian term. It refers to the potential of a cultural movement to express the hegemonic line of the dominant class.
79. Bruno Gabrielli, "Una esperienza con Aldo Rossi," in Salvatore Farinato, ed., Per Aldo Rossi (Venice: Marsilio, 1997), p. 34.
80. Giorgio Piccinato, Vieri Quilici, Manfredo Tafuri, "La città-territorio verso una nuova dimensione," Casabella continuità 270 (1963), pp. 16–25.
81. The category of the city-territory was initially "institutionalized" within the Italian urban debate at an important conference organized by Giancarlo de Carlo and the Istituto Lombardo per gli Studi Economici e Sociali (ILSES) in the town of Stresa on Lake Maggiore in January 1962 under the title of "The New Dimension of the City." Many protagonists of the Arezzo workshop (which took place the following

year) participated, including Rossi. Indeed, the Arezzo workshop was conceived as a follow-up to the conference in Stresa. See Giancarlo de Carlo et al., La nuova dimensione della città: La città-ragione (Milan: ILSES, 1962).
82. Claudio Greppi and Alberto Pedrolli, "Produzione e programmazione territoriale," in Quaderni rossi 3 (1963), pp. 94–101.
83. "Casa a chi lavora" (housing for those who work) was the main slogan of housing programs such as INA-Casa.
84. Greppi and Pedrolli, "Produzione e programmazione territoriale," p. 95.
85. Ibid., p. 95.
86. Greppi made the following observation in an interview with the author in October 2007: "At the time of the publication of his [early] writings and his major book L'architettura della città, Rossi was not yet known for his projects, but more for an idiosyncratic reading of the city based on urban geography. The latter was irreducible to the blind technocratic approaches that were fashionable at that time—those of the city-territory and townscape, on the one hand, and the megastructure on the other."
87. Aldo Rossi, The Architecture of the City, trans. Diane Ghirardo and Joan Ockman (Cambridge, MA: MIT Press, 1982), p. 103.
88. Rossi's idea to title his book L'architettura della città, which summarizes the thrust of his theoretical investigations at the end of the 1950s and especially in the early 1960s, was inspired by Ceccarelli. According to Ceccarelli, Rossi's initial idea was to publish the lectures on typology he had given as Aymonino's assistant in the course "Caratteri distributivi degli edifici" (Organizational characteristics of buildings) under the title "La città come fondamento per lo studio degli edifici" (The city as a foundation for the study of buildings), which was also the title of one of the lectures. In 1963–64 Ceccarelli had translated into Italian Kevin's Lynch book The Image of the City while he was studying at MIT and in close contact with Lynch, and he had it printed by Marsilio, the small publishing house he had cofounded two years earlier. Ceccarelli reported his discovery of Lynch to Rossi and proposed to his friend that he write a book for Marsilio with the same ambitious scope. It is worthwhile to recall the story of Marsilio since it represents an interesting convergence of urban culture and Operaism. Marsilio (the name refers to an important fourteenth-century Paduan philosopher and jurist who was a harsh critic of the temporal power of the Catholic Church) was established in 1961 by a small group of young Paduan intellectuals that included, besides Ceccarelli, Antonio Negri. These intellectuals were involved at the time in the Catholic movement Intesa, a section of the Federazione Universitaria Cattolici Italiani (FUCI); at the same time they were influenced by Panzieri's critique of neocapitalism (Panzieri would subsequently co-opt Negri into the group around Quaderni rossi). Marsilio's aim was to address Italy's

industrial transformations and provide innovative theoretical frameworks for its critical interpretation. Both Lynch's Image of the City and Rossi's L'architettura della città fell within this editorial line. But if the publication of Lynch's book coincided with the optimism of the early 1960s, Rossi's book was colored by the beginning of the economic and political crisis that began in Italy between 1964 and 1965. It is interesting to note that Ceccarelli also proposed to publish the book by Rossi because he felt that Rossi's "multidisciplinary" approach would not be able to find a proper editorial home among the more traditional and more specialized publishers. Interview with Paolo Ceccarelli by the author, October 2007.
89. Aldo Rossi, Gianugo Polesello, Emilio Mattioni, and Luciano Semerani, "Città e territorio negli aspetti funzionali e figurativi della pianificazione continua," in Atti del X convegno dell'Istituto Nazionale di Urbanistica (Trieste: INU, 1965), pp. 286–300.
90. Ibid., p. 290.
91. Ibid., p. 292.
92. Ibid.
93. Gianugo Polesello, "Ab initio, indagatio initiorum: Ricordi e confessioni," in Pisana Posocco, Gemma Radicchio, and Gundula Rakowitz, eds., Care architetture (Turin: Umberto Allemandi, 2002), p. 16.
94. Rossi, The Architecture of the City, p. 116 (my italics).
95. Ibid.
96. Claudio Greppi has recalled that the project was born out the growing interest of the Florentine students of architecture in Panzieri and Tronti's Autonomist Marxism. The Florentine section of Classe operaia was the largest among the different regional groups in Italy, and it was made up mostly of architecture students. According to Greppi: "The school of architecture was, at that time, the ideal place to develop a broader critique of the capitalist city that would involve and combine politics and a vision of the city and its project. Against the imperative of reforming and rationalizing the city, we started to think that the time had come simply to critique the existing one. My diploma project was strongly inspired by the large-scale designs of the mid-1960s, but instead of presenting some colorful utopian vision of the future city, I was critically exaggerating the mechanism of the existing one. We thought that the architect was not at all suited for agit-prop, that the best he could do was side with capitalist power and work on 'wrong projects.' Our adhesion to Operaism was the rejection of any populist and activist stance that would eventually result in designing social housing projects, or case del popolo. Against these temptations Tronti clearly warned us: for the working class it is more useful to be a great reactionary than some petit-bourgeois revolutionary." Interview with the author, September 2007.
97. This hypothesis is bolstered by the fact that Greppi is in close contact with members of Archizoom such as Corretti and Morozzi, who,

87

according to Greppi, were regular participants in the meetings organized by Classe operaia in Florence.

98. This episode is also recalled by Andrea Branzi in his recent comments on the republication of Archizoom's No-Stop City. See Andrea Branzi, ed., No-Stop City, Archizoom Associati (HYX: Orléans, 2006), pp. 142–43.

99. Archizoom, "Città, catena di montaggio del sociale: Ideologia e teoria della metropoli," in Branzi, No-Stop City, Archizoom Associati, pp. 156–57. Originally published in Casabella 350–51 (1970), pp. 22–34.

100. Archizoom existed from 1966 to 1974. After the dissolution of the group, all its members enjoyed successful careers as industrial designers and worked with major Italian companies.

101. "Città, catena di montaggio del sociale: Ideologia e teoria della metropoli," pp. 160–61.

102. Ibid., p. 161.

103. Ibid., p. 173.

104. Ludwig Hilberseimer, Entfaltung einer Planungsidee (Berlin: Bauwelt Fundamente, 1963); Ludwig Hilberseimer, Una idea di piano, introduction and translation by Giorgio Grassi (Padua: Marsilio, 1967). Note that the book was published in the series "Polis," directed by Rossi for the Marsilio publishing house. Hilberseimer is also the most frequently cited architect in Grassi's most important book, La costruzione logica dell'architettura, published by Marsilio in 1967.

105. Andrea Branzi, postscript, in No-Stop City, Archizoom Associati, pp. 148–49.

106. Tafuri, "Toward a Critique of Architectural Ideology," in Hays, ed., Architecture Theory since 1968, p. 22.

107. See especially Branzi's "revisionist" interpretation of No-Stop City as an early manifestation of a "weak and diffuse modernity," in Andrea Branzi, Weak and Diffuse: A World of Projects at the Beginning of the 21st Century (Milan: Skira, 2006).

108. Branzi, postscript, in No-Stop City, Archizoom Associati, p. 142.

109. The tragic epilogue of arrests and false accusations of members of the Autonomia movement in the 1970s occurred after the movement had already suffered internal defections, strong divisions, and ideological collapses. This history of the "radical" 1970s has been very much suppressed by the many apologetic voices today.

110. See Germano Celant, "Radical Architecture," in Emilio Ambasz, ed., Italy: The New Domestic Landscape: Achievements and Problems of Italian Design (New York: Museum of Modern Art; and Florence: Centro Di, 1972), pp. 380–87. The photograph of the gorilla that appears on the cover of Casabella 367 (1972) came from a specimen in the Akeley Hall of African Mammals in the American Museum of Natural History in New York.

111. As Toraldo di Francia stated in an e-mail exchange with the author, May 2007.

112. Mario Tronti, Operai e capitale, p. 265.

Credits

1 Photograph: Silvestro Loconsolo. Courtesy Silvestro Loconsolo
4 Photographer unknown. Courtesy Archive of Centro Gobetti, Turin
5 Photographer unknown. Courtesy Fondazione Aldo Rossi, Milan
6 Photographer unknown. Courtesy Andrea Branzi
7 Photographer unknown. Courtesy Fondazione Aldo Rossi, Milan
14, 15, 21, 22, 28, 29, 40, 41 Courtesy Avery Architectural and Fine Arts Library, Columbia University
26 Courtesy Fondazione Aldo Rossi, Milan
27 Courtesy Fondazione Aldo Rossi, Milan
30 Courtesy Fondazione Aldo Rossi, Milan
35 Courtesy Claudio Greppi
36 Courtesy Claudio Greppi
37 Courtesy Andrea Branzi
38 Courtesy Andrea Branzi
39 Courtesy Andrea Branzi
42 Courtesy Museum of Modern Art / Art Resource, NY

1 Workers at a debate about the renewal of
their contracts at the IBM plant in Vimercate,
Italy, 1969. Photograph: Silvestro Loconsolo.
The issue of wages and the independence of
workers' salaries from the costs of production
was regarded by Operaist militants as the
ultimate political weapon against capitalism. For
the Operaists capitalism was not only an unjust
process of accumulation but an institutionalized
form of political control established through the
increasingly pervasive and diffuse organization
of work itself. The workers' ultimate political
challenge to capitalism was to ask to be paid
more money to work less.

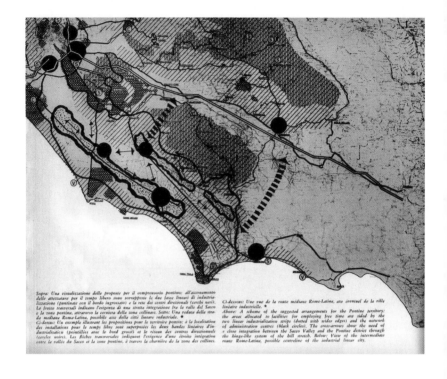

2 AUA (Architetti Urbanisti Associati: Vieri Quilici, Giorgio Piccinato, Enrico Fattinanzi, and Manfredo Tafuri), city-territory project in the Pontine district near Rome, showing production and business centers. The advent of the welfare state and its new geography of production is represented as expanding the production system beyond the factory and over the entire territory. In Italy and Europe in the late 1950s and early 1960s production was no longer confined to the factory but extended to the whole cycle of urban life: work, leisure, welfare, culture.

ARTE FUTURISTA

La prospettiva del comunismo (da "il Pioniere dell'Unità")

3 Reprint of a comic strip in the seventh issue of the Operaist journal Classe operaia, 1964. It originally appeared in Pioniere dell'Unità, a supplement to the Communist Party newspaper L'Unità. It was reprinted with the caption "Futurist Art—the Communist perspective," and exemplifies the techno-utopianism of the institutional Left, which envisioned new technology as engendering an Eden of work. The comic strip narrates the story of "Atomino," who is trying to rationalize work in his factory. It concludes with a view of the factory as a holiday village. Though naive, this comic strip conceived by the Communist Party illustrates the rise of capitalist biopower over the working class in the subtle form of workers' welfare. The Operaists and Autonomists attacked this "progressive" vision, which they saw as a reactionary response to the intensifying workers' struggle.

4 The Operaists at an editorial meeting of
Quaderni rossi, Turin, 1962. Photographer
unknown. Present were Antonio Negri (third
from left), Mario Tronti (second from right),
and Raniero Panzieri (right). Panzieri, Tronti,
and Negri were the key figures in the Operaist
movement and represent its three main
moments: the critique of technology (Panzieri),
the theoretical foundation of workers' power
(Tronti), and workers' autonomy (Negri).

5 The "Venice Group," 1964. Photographer
unknown. The original nucleus of the group
consisted of Aldo Rossi (center) and Carlo
Aymonino (right). This group was responsible
for bringing back the study of the city
and urban theory as a form of political and
cultural commitment.

6 Archizoom Associati in front of the
group's studio, Via Ricaboli, Florence, 1968.
Photographer unknown. Archizoom formed
as a parody of the British group Archigram.
Instead of faith in technological progress, their
work displayed a cynical and politicized attitude
toward the city's evolution, seen as a final clash
between workers and capital. Left to right: Paolo
Deganello, Lucia Bartolini, Massimo Morozzi,
Natalino Torniani (associated collaborator),
Dario Bartolini, Gilberto Corretti, Andrea Branzi.

7 Individuals associated with the Tendenza,
Milan, 1973. Photographer unknown. This
photograph was taken before the opening of
the Fifteenth Triennale of Milan, devoted to
the theme of "Architettura Razionale." The
group is standing in front of a mural by Arduino
Cantafora depicting "exemplary" buildings

designed by Ludwig Hilberseimer, Adolf Loos,
Gunnar Asplund, and Alessandro Antonelli,
montaged to create an ideal "socialist city."
Left to right: Richard Meier, Julia Bloomfield,
Peter Carl, Vittorio Savi, Paolo Rizzato, Antonio
Monestiroli, Max Bosshard, Aldo Rossi,
Arduino Cantafora, Gianni Braghieri, Bruno
Reichlin, Aldo Aymonino, Fabio Reinhardt,
Heinrich Helfenstein, Jos Da Nobrega, Franco
Raggi, Claudio Maneri, Massimo Scolari,
Michael Graves. The Tendenza originated in
Milan around Rossi and became a transnational
network of architects. The attendees were
mostly from Italy, Switzerland, Spain, Portugal,
Germany, and the United States. Those from
Spain and Portugal were most politicized
and embraced Rossi's ideas in the context of
political turmoil in their own countries provoked
by waning Fascist regimes.

8 Quaderni rossi 2, 1962. This journal was founded by Raniero Panzieri in 1961. It ran for only six issues, ceasing publication in 1965. Its central themes were the capitalist organization of work and the possibility of workers' autonomy. The second issue, published in 1962, opened with Mario Tronti's seminal essay "La fabbrica e la società," in which the author theorized the role of production as the core of capitalist civilization. According to Tronti, production was no longer just one part of the economic cycle confined to the factory, but an essential form of capitalism pervading the whole spectrum of social relationships.

9,10 Classe operaia 1 and 3 (1964). Founded by Mario Tronti in 1964 as a monthly journal dedicated to the cause of "struggling workers," Classe operaia was produced by Operaists who split off from the Quaderni rossi group at the end of 1963. The last issue appeared in 1966. The two approaches of the journal were exemplified by editorials published in two of the early issues: Tronti's seminal "manifesto" "Lenin in Inghilterra" called for a Leninist use of the party organization within advanced capitalist society; and Antonio Negri's "Operai senza alleati" argued for self-organized forms of struggle.

11 Contropiano 2 (1971). Contropiano was founded by Alberto Asor Rosa, Massimo Cacciari, and Antonio Negri in 1968 and published until 1971. Negri left the journal after the first issue. This journal concluded the theoretical trajectory of Operaismo. Unlike Classe operaia, its focus was more on theory than direct intervention. The most significant contribution was without doubt Cacciari's "Sulla genesi del pensiero negativo," a genealogy of the ideological mechanism through which the bourgeoisie internalized capitalism's cultural and political crises. Architecture and the city were treated in the journal as a field of political analysis, addressed in contributions by members of the newly formed Institute of History at the IUAV, Venice's school of architecture. Manfredo Tafuri's analysis of the relationship between the ideology of "Austro-Marxism" and the politics of social housing in Vienna after World War I exemplified the themes and interests of the journal in relation to architecture.

12, 13 Mario Tronti's Operai e capitale (1966) was the seminal book of Operaismo and the main source for 1970s Autonomia movements. It was published at the end of Classe operaia's existence, when Tronti considered the political experiment of the journal to be at risk of becoming a marginal avant-garde initiative rather than an agent of real politics. In this book Tronti republished his interventions in Quaderni rossi and Classe operaia, adding a new section on the central theme of his research: "Marx, Labor Force, Working Class." The book consists of three parts. The first includes essays published in the socialist journal Mondoperaio and in Quaderni rossi; it deals with the rediscovery of Marx beyond Marxism and the process of integration of society within the productive space of capitalism. The second part includes the polemical texts published in Classe operaia and addresses questions of political organization of the new working class. The third part focuses on relations among the working class as theorized in Marx, the nature of its power as a labor force, and its political constitution as an autonomous class with its own interests. Here the concept of autonomy reaches its most radical conclusion: in order to take power, the working class must refuse not capitalism but capital's most essential premise, work itself. In a revised edition of 1971, Tronti added a section on the struggles of the American working class, seen as more advanced than its European counterpart by virtue of being devoid of ideology. After Operaismo, Tronti further radicalized his position in his studies on working-class politics, summarizing his argument in the book Sull'autonomia del politico (1977), based on a seminar delivered in 1972.

14 Casabella continuità, special issue on Adolf Loos, 1959. Casabella continuità (1953–65) was refounded by Ernesto Nathan Rogers from the original Casabella established by Giuseppe Pagano in 1928. Rogers's intention was to reinforce the relationship between the practice of architecture and its theoretical discourse by addressing broad themes of philosophy and politics. Rogers supported the contributions of his students and assistants at the Milan Politecnico, including Aldo Rossi and Vittorio Gregotti. Besides writing on architects such as Peter Behrens and Le Corbusier, and on books such as Hans Sedlmayr's Verlust der Mitte and Emil Kaufmann's Von Ledoux bis Le Corbusier, Rossi edited a special issue in 1959 entirely devoted to Loos, who at that time was still considered a secondary figure of the Modern Movement. Loos was key to Rossi's reinterpretation of the legacy of rationalism and a way to move beyond its image of "functionalism"

and "International Style." Rossi's interest in Loos and the Viennese cultural context may be seen as comparable to Operaismo's interest in figures like Gustav Mahler and Robert Musil, the only two nonpolitical thinkers cited in Tronti's Operai e capitale.

15 Casabella continuità, special issue on young Italian architects, 1963. Most of the architects featured were in their thirties and active in Milan and Venice. The magazine's cover shows a section drawing of the austere Monument to the Partisan in Cuneo by Aldo Rossi, Luca Meda, and Gianugo Polesello (1962). As Rossi himself admitted, his early work, inspired by both the abstract aesthetics of Max Bill and the monumentality of Stalinist architecture, was highly provocative for its stubborn use of extremely simplified forms at a time when such imagery was mostly identified with either totalitarianism or bureaucratic capitalism.

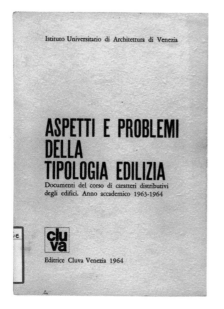

Istituto Universitario di Architettura di Venezia

ASPETTI E PROBLEMI DELLA TIPOLOGIA EDILIZIA

Documenti del corso di caratteri distributivi
degli edifici. Anno accademico 1963-1964

cluva

Editrice Cluva Venezia 1964

Istituto Universitario di Architettura di Venezia

LA FORMAZIONE DEL CONCETTO DI TIPOLOGIA EDILIZIA

Atti del corso di caratteri distributivi degli edifici
Anno accademico 1964-1965

cluva

Editrice Cluva Venezia 1965

16, 17 Course booklets prepared at the IUAV and published by Cluva, 1965. During the academic years 1963–64 and 1964–65, Rossi joined Carlo Aymonino as assistant professor in Aymonino's newly established program at the IUAV, "Organizational Characteristics of Buildings." Prior to this, Rossi had carried out research on Milanese residential typologies. In their collaboration, Rossi and Aymonino further developed the typological analysis of the city that Rossi had initiated, building up the theoretical premises of what later would become one of the main themes of the "Scuola di Venezia": the relationship between the city's visible and material form (morphology) and its inner structure (typology). The two seminal course booklets published at the conclusion of each course in 1963 and 1964, on aspects and problems of building typology and the formation of the concept of building typology respectively, exemplify the method applied by Aymonino and Rossi, which was to prepare their classes by writing theoretical and methodological essays. This represented a challenge to the traditional pedagogy at schools of architecture, where teaching was based on practical issues and separated from academic instruction in history and urbanism. Against this, Rossi and Aymonino emphasized typology as a theoretical and "autonomous" bridge between architecture, urbanism, and urban history. Rossi's contribution to the IUAV courses and booklets would become the core of his book L'architettura della città.

18 Aldo Rossi, L'architettura della città, 1966. Written by Rossi between 1963 and 1965 while teaching in Venice with Carlo Aymonino, the book originated as notes for Rossi's classes and the articles he had published in Casabella. It was assembled with editorial assistance from Rossi's wife, the actress Sonia Gessner. The book is divided into four parts. In the first part, Rossi summarizes the overarching principle of his theory, the dialectical unity between the urban artifact and typological knowledge of the city. In the second part, he outlines a new methodology of urban analysis, introducing concepts such as the study area, and provides a basic classification of the primary elements that constitute urban phenomena; a fundamental case study is Berlin, whose urban history Rossi had previously treated in Casabella.

In the third part, the most important of the book, Rossi introduces his crucial concept of *locus*, which has to do with the singularity of the urban place and thus the primary role of geography in understanding the city. The concept of *locus* opposes abstract urban categories that were fashionable at the time such as planning and environment. In the last part, Rossi analyzes the economic and political modalities by which urban phenomena evolve. The book clearly reflects an effort on the part of Rossi and Aymonino to unify architecture, urbanism, and history in the interest of a general assessment of the city seen as a relationship between its physical form and deeper structures.

LUDWIG
HILBERSEIMER

collana Polis / Marsilio Editori

UN' IDEA
DI PIANO

19, 20 The history of so-called autonomous architecture consists more of editorial undertakings—books, magazines, translations of important books on architecture and urbanism—than of actual buildings. Following the instant success of Rossi's <u>L'architettura della città</u>, Rossi himself initiated a series of books emblematically called Polis, with the aim of publishing books or writings by architects that reinforced the link between the city and politics. The series was launched with Rossi's translation of Etienne-Louis Boullée's <u>Essai sur l'art</u>, and included Giorgio Grassi's <u>La costruzione logica dell'architettura</u> (1967); Carlo Aymonino's <u>Origini e sviluppo della città moderna</u> (1967), originally published in the

journal Critica Marxista as a polemical answer to Leonardo Benevolo's Le origini dell'urbanistica moderna (1967); and Ludovico Quaroni's La torre di babele (1967). Emblematic of the series and of Rossi's editorial project were the translation of Ludwig Hilberseimer's Entfaltung einer Planungsidee in 1967 as Un'idea di piano, edited by Giorgio Grassi; and of the collected writings of Hannes Meyer in 1969, under the title Architettura o rivoluzione, edited by Francesco Dal Co. These translations attest to Rossi's commitment to reconsider the legacy of the Modern Movement not in terms of stylistic phenomena but as theoretical and political projects.

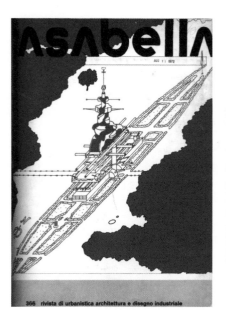 

21, 22 Casabella 366 and 367 (1972). After Rogers's expulsion as Casabella's editorial director in 1964, the magazine again took on importance between 1970 and 1976 under the direction of the industrial designer Alessandro Mendini. Mendini quickly became the mentor of the Florentine groups Superstudio and Archizoom, and their existence and activity coincided with his tenure. Under Mendini, Casabella aimed to connect social and political issues that had emerged in the aftermath of 1968–69 with neo-avant-garde movements like Minimalism, Conceptualism, and Arte Povera. In 1972 he celebrated the international triumph of contemporary Italian design in the exhibition "Italy: The New Domestic Landscape," held at the Museum of Modern Art in New York, with two emblematic covers. The May issue depicted a military ship crossing the Atlantic. The June issue featured a gorilla reproduced from a postcard sent to Mendini from New York by Superstudio; Mendini added the label "Radical Design," taken from art critic Germano Celant's contribution to the MoMA catalogue. The label spelled the movement's institutionalization, and with this publication the members of Superstudio and Archizoom realized their project had come to an end.

23 Controspazio, special issue on the Fifteenth Triennale in Milan, 1973. Founded in 1969 by Paolo Portoghesi in the wake of the 1968–69 student protests in Italian schools of architecture, Controspazio (1969–80) was dominated by two young architects and theorists, Ezio Bonfanti and Massimo Scolari, and influenced by Aldo Rossi. Unlike Mendini's Casabella, Controspazio focused on the discipline of architecture itself, but with a specifically political approach. Its main theme was the reinvention of a rationalist tradition in response to the crisis of modernism. Within this perspective, it devoted monographic issues to topics such as the Bauhaus and Russian Constructivism. It soon became the magazine of the Tendenza, in 1973 giving an entire issue to the Triennale, which was curated by Rossi.

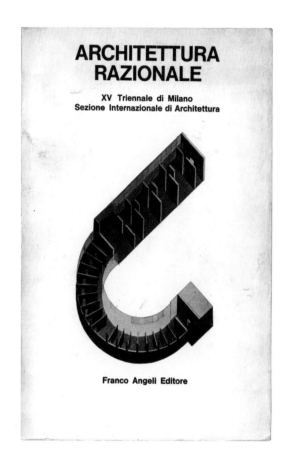

ARCHITETTURA
RAZIONALE

XV Triennale di Milano
Sezione Internazionale di Architettura

Franco Angeli Editore

24 Architettura razionale, 1973. Published within a series edited by Massimo Scolari for the Milan publisher Franco Angeli, this book supported the Fifteenth Triennale by offering a series of theoretical texts and projects by important figures of the Modern Movement such as Adolf Behne, Hans Schmidt, Ludwig Hilberseimer, and Hannes Meyer; and by young Italian theorists such as Scolari and Ezio Bonfanti. The book also includes projects by European and American "neorationalist" architects and students from Italian, Swiss, Spanish, and German schools. One of the Tendenza's objectives was to influence schools of architecture through collective research programs and urban projects.

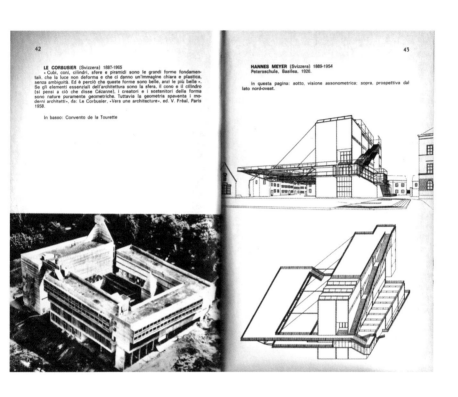

LE CORBUSIER (Svizzera) 1887-1965
« Cubi, coni, cilindri, sfere e piramidi sono le grandi forme fondamentali, che la luce non deforma e che ci danno un'immagine chiara e plastica, senza ambiguità. Ed è perciò che queste forme sono belle, anzi le più belle ». Se gli elementi essenziali dell'architettura sono la sfera, il cono e il cilindro (si pensi a ciò che disse Cézanne), i creatori e i sostenitori della forma sono nature puramente geometriche. Tuttavia la geometria spaventa i moderni architetti», da: Le Corbusier, «Vers une architecture», ed. V. Fréal, Paris 1958.

In basso: Convento de la Tourette

HANNES MEYER (Svizzera) 1889-1954
Peterschule, Basilea. 1926.

In questa pagina: sotto, visione assonometrica; sopra, prospettiva dal lato nord-ovest.

25 This spread from <u>Architettura razionale</u> shows two canonical buildings of European rationalism, Le Corbusier's monastery at La Tourette and Hannes Meyer's Peterschule. Far from rejecting the Modern Movement and its legacy, Rossi and the neorationalist architects around him embraced it by promoting rigorous architectural analysis with the aim of defining a vocabulary common to "exemplary" existing buildings. La Tourette was also the subject of an intense review by Rossi for Rogers's <u>Casabella</u>.

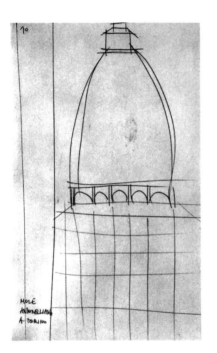

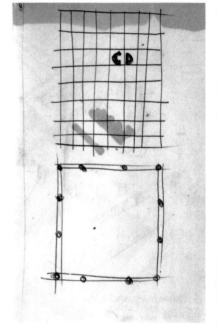

26, 27 Aldo Rossi, sketches for competition project for an administrative center in Turin, 1962. Rossi and his teammates Luca Meda and Gianugo Polesello took part in this important competition for the new *centro direzionale*, conceived as a response to the emergent urban phenomena of the city-territory and the service sector's increasing hegemony in Turin. Rossi's sketches show the Roman grid of Turin juxtaposed with the dome of Alessandro Antonelli's Mole, built in the second half of the nineteenth century, and with his proposed plan for the new building.

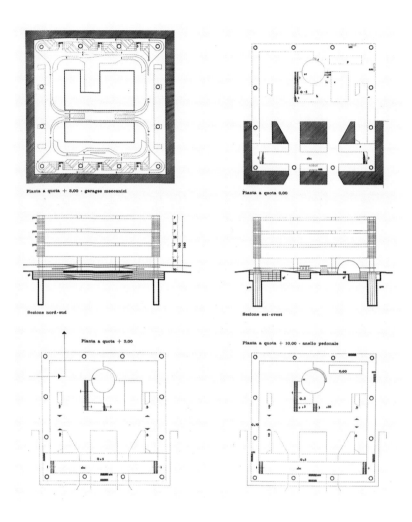

Pianta a quota + 3,00 - garages meccanici

Pianta a quota 0,00

Sezione nord-sud

Sezione est-ovest

Pianta a quota + 3,00

Pianta a quota + 10,00 - anello pedonale

28 Aldo Rossi, Luca Meda, and Gianugo Polesello, competition board for the *centro direzionale*, Turin, 1962. Plans and sections. Against the techno-utopian character of many projects proposed for this competition, Rossi, Meda, and Polesello proposed a polemical approach in which the complexity of the program was reduced to a very simple form intended as "exceptional" within the city and as analogous to Turin's grid. The project is monumental in scale; however, its compact form was seen as a way to avoid the dispersion of administrative activities throughout the city.

29 Aldo Rossi, Luca Meda, and Gianugo
Polesello, competition entry for *centro
direzionale*, Turin, 1962. Model

30 Aldo Rossi, Gallaratese housing block, near Milan, 1967–70. Carlo Aymonino invited Rossi to design part of a social housing complex he was in charge of on the outskirts of Milan. For Rossi this was an occasion to summarize the principles of his design method, which consisted of the use and composition of typological elements based on existing forms like the gallery. Rossi's aim was to liberate the city from redundant architectural imagery and to propose a simplified and schematic architecture that would act more as a frame and background for life than a representation of it.

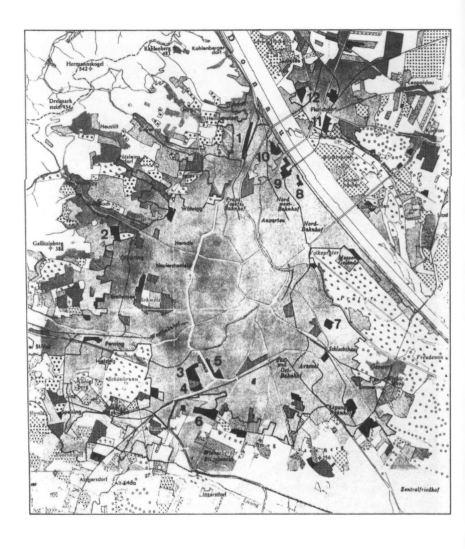

31 "Red Vienna," from Oswald Mathias
Ungers's article "Die Wiener Superblocks,"
Werk 4 (1970). The 1960s and early 1970s saw a
rediscovery across Europe of the social housing
blocks promoted by the municipality of Vienna
between the beginning of the 1920s and Hitler's
annexation of Austria. Interest in this overlooked
chapter of modern urbanism reflected the
search for a historical example of architectural
form and urban design that represented the
working class no longer as completely absorbed
by capitalism's homogenizing logic but as
a political exception to it. Rossi, Aymonino,
Panzieri, and Tronti celebrated the residential
superblocks in Vienna as exemplary forms of the
socialist city, while Tafuri criticized them as an
excess of "built ideology."

32 Peter Behrens, Winarskyhof, Vienna,
1924–25. Designed in collaboration with Josef
Frank, Margarete Lihotzky, Oskar Strnad, Josef
Hoffmann, and Adolf Loos, the project was built
in conjunction with the Red Vienna program.

33 Ludwig Hilberseimer, project for a Vertical City, 1924. Perspective from an east-west street. In the mid-1960s Hilberseimer became a cult figure among young Italian architects for his austere formal vocabulary and his sophisticated writings on the city. The German architect's uncompromising position on the capitalist city resulted in sharp and precise observations on the metropolis, contrasting with the more romantic and visionary celebrations of protagonists of the Modern Movement like Le Corbusier. Hilberseimer's Vertical City would be a fundamental point of departure for Archizoom's No-Stop City project; the young Florentine group admired its total absence of drama and its abstraction. In 1970, presenting their early hypothesis for No-Stop City in Casabella, Archizoom quoted a passage from Thomas Mann's novel Royal Highness (1909): "The time is noon on an ordinary weekday; the season of the year does not matter. The weather is fair to moderate. It is not raining, but the sky is not clear; it is a uniform light gray, uninteresting and somber, and the street lies in a dull and sober light which robs it of all mystery, all individuality."

34 Ludwig Hilberseimer, standing in front of a
model of a skyscraper composed of six stacked-
up units of his Welfare City, 1928

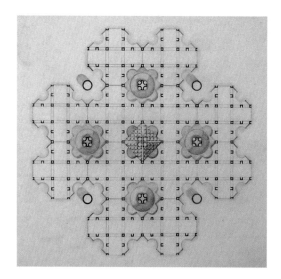

35, 36 Claudio Greppi, diploma project for a territorial factory near Prato, Italy, 1964–65. General plan and typical plan of one unit. A militant member of Mario Tronti's group Classe Operaia and later of Potere Operaio (Worker's Power), Greppi assimilated Frederick Engels's thesis that there is no such thing as a working-class city, only a working-class critique of the existing city, and took up Tronti's hypothesis of society as a factory. His diploma project radicalized the expansion of the production-consumption network by proposing the factory itself as the "real" form of the contemporary city. Also inspired by Louis Kahn's architecture and Kenzo Tange's 1960 plan for Tokyo, Greppi's project reduced the city to its vertical and horizontal infrastructure. Unlike its references, the project had no progressivist or humanistic aspirations, only that of making visible the urban conditions imposed by capitalism. It would be a crucial inspiration for Archizoom's No-Stop City.

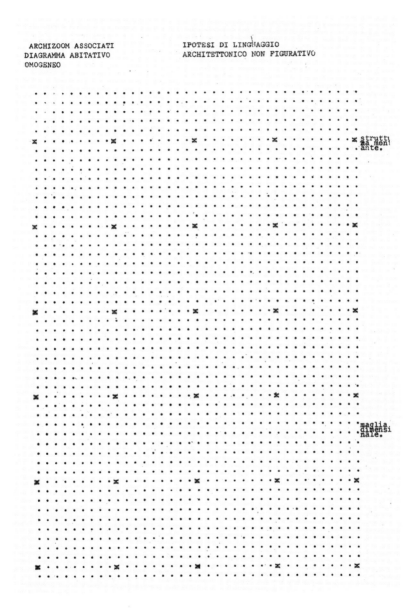

ARCHIZOOM ASSOCIATI
DIAGRAMMA ABITATIVO
OMOGENEO

IPOTESI DI LINGUAGGIO
ARCHITETTONICO NON FIGURATIVO

37 Archizoom, No-Stop City, 1968–70. Diagram of a homogeneous habitat. If Greppi's project for a factory-city still had reminiscences of the figurative forms of Louis Kahn, Archizoom's No-Stop City, pursuing Hilberseimer's research into a totally abstract architecture,

presents a hypothesis for a nonfigurative architectural-urban language. Typed as a field of dots, this early drawing reduces the city to its infrastructural capacity to reproduce labor: "a lift every 100 square meters, a bathroom every 50 square meters."

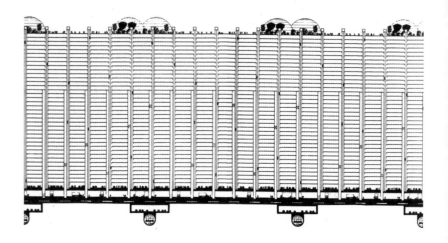

38 Archizoom Associati, No-Stop City, 1968–70.
Section of the city. The project was initially
conceived as a reelaboration and radicalization
of Hilberseimer's Vertical City. Activities are
stacked vertically and continuously, and all
representational imagery is suppressed. As
Archizoom wrote polemically in Domus in 1971,
"The city no longer 'represents' the system
but becomes the system itself, programmed
and isotropic."

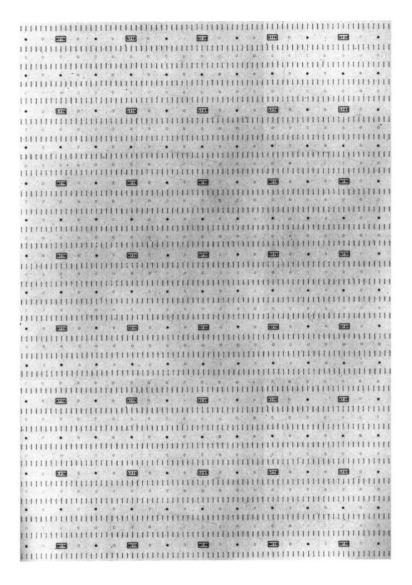

39 Archizoom, No-Stop City, 1968–70. Drawing
showing the residential area designed as both a
parking lot and a supermarket. Commenting on
No-Stop City's genesis, Andrea Branzi writes,
"The originality of the Archizoom group lay
precisely in the fact that it connected socialist
realism and Pop art, because both issued from a
radical and extreme stance, wherein the contents
of the political avant-gardes overlapped with
those of the artistic avant-gardes. Working-
classism and consumerism, Mario Tronti and
Andy Warhol: opposite worlds but not so
remote ... both obeyed the materialist logic of
'more money and less work.'"

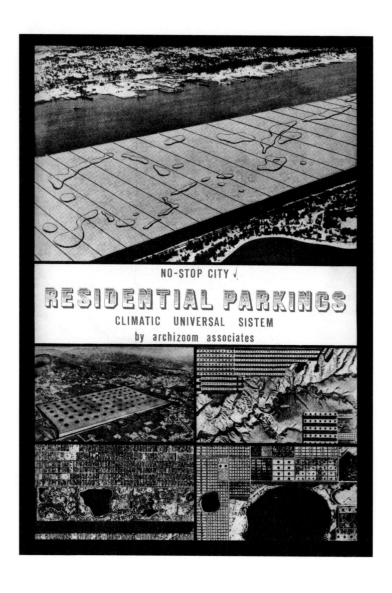

NO-STOP CITY √

RESIDENTIAL PARKINGS

CLIMATIC UNIVERSAL SISTEM

by archizoom associates

40, 41 Archizoom, No-Stop City, 1968–70. Plates from the project's publication in <u>Domus</u>, March 1971. The members of Archizoom presented themselves as "Stalinist" architects and on several public occasions even satirically endorsed censorship of the many "avant-garde" and "utopian" projects that proliferated in architectural magazines and exhibitions starting in the mid-1960s, "in order to limit the potentially unnecessary panic that would spread among the population" if they were to be built. In 1971 they presented for the first time their research for a

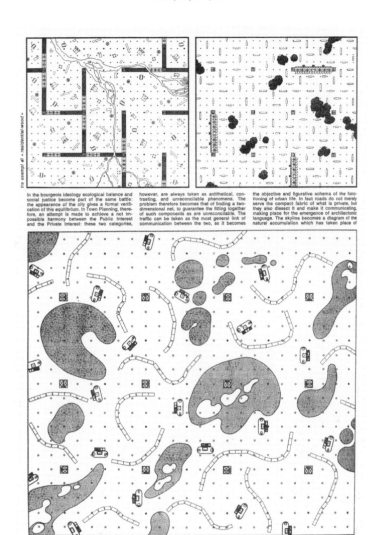

In the bourgeois ideology ecological balance and social justice become part of the same battle: the appearance of the city gives a formal verification of this equilibrium. In Town Planning, therefore, an attempt is made to achieve a not impossible harmony between the Public Interest and the Private Interest: these two categories, however, are always taken as antithetical, contrasting, and unreconcilable phenomena. The problem therefore becomes that of finding a two-dimensional net, to guarantee the fitting together of such components as are unreconcilable. The traffic can be taken as the most general link of communication between the two, as it becomes the objective and figurative schema of the functioning of urban life. In fact roads do not merely serve the compact fabric of what is private, but they also dissect it and make it communicating, making place for the emergence of architectonic language. The skyline becomes a diagram of the natural accumulation which has taken place of

homogeneous habitat in the form of "residential parking areas." The habitat was intended to be composed of nothing but generic architectural signs, thus divesting it of all technological enthusiasm and focusing on the essential aspects of capitalism's integration of urban space. According to Archizoom, only by demonstrating the consequences of this integration was it possible to conceive of the working class's autonomy—no longer as the workers' resistance to the space of production, but as their appropriation of it.

42, 43 Installation views of the exhibitions "Italy: The New Domestic Landscape," Museum of Modern Art, New York, 1972, showing outdoor display cases for "Objects" section; and the Fifteenth Triennale, Milan, 1973, with visionary city model by Leon and Robert Krier. The beginning of the 1970s brought international acclaim and canonization to Italian design.

These two exhibitions were the main vehicles for this. They made the theoretical work of the two contemporary movements—the neo-avant-garde Radicals and the neorationalist Tendenza into successful "postmodernist" styles, albeit at the cost of altering, if not entirely removing, their political *raisons d'être*.